The Complete Cycle Sport Guide

In the same series:

The Complete Windsurfing Guide
* The Complete Microlight Guide
* The Complete Hang Gliding Guide

* *in preparation*

Peter Konopka

The
Complete
CYCLE
SPORT
Guide

EP PUBLISHING LIMITED

Dr Peter Konopka studied medicine at universities in Erlangen, Tübingen and Munich, hence his special attention to the maintenance of health through movement therapy and healthy diet. A logical result of his medical and sporting interests was his appointment as medical officer to the *Bund Deutscher Radfahrer* (West German National Cycling Federation), and his links with other sporting bodies. Since 1972 he has looked after the BDR national road and cyclo-cross teams. He has already had published several books, articles and papers, many of which have dealt with correct sporting diet. He has also collaborated on the cycling periodical *Tour*. Dr Konopka is himself an active racing cyclist, and in 1979 he was Schwabian champion in his age class.

Picture credits
E. Baumann p. 112
R. Behrbohm p. 30, 31, 34, 35, 38, 39, 40, 43, 45, 46, 47, 49, 50, 51, 53, 55, 58, 61, 66, 118–121, 133, 135
D. Birkner (blv Archiv-Sport) p. 17, 73, 81, 112, 113, 123, 177
H. Dargel p. 4, 47, 59
Elegance Pro Domo p. 17
W. Gronen p. 11, 12, 13, 23, 41, 110
K. W. Hochschorner p. 52
E. Kahlich p. 18, 19, 20, 21, 26, 27, 36, 37, 41, 42, 43, 44, 45, 52, 54, 55, 56, 57, 58, 63, 66, 72, 78, 79, 84, 93, 107, 110, 113, 131, 135, 138, 149, 159, 171, 179, 180, 181, 182
Keiper Dynavit GmbH p. 136
P. Konopka p. 41, 48, 56
M. Mühlberger p. 2/3, 69, 87, 91, 127, 154, 163
H.-A. Roth p. 108
Shimano (Europa) GmbH p. 19, 27, 31, 34, 44
H. Sonderhüsken p. 22, 82, 83, 109, 111, 114
F. Wöllzenmüller p. 65, 134

Originally published in German under the title *Radsport vom Anfänger bis zum Könner* Copyright © 1981 BLV Verlagsgesellschaft mbH, Munich

First English edition 1982
English translation copyright © 1982
EP Publishing Limited
ISBN 0 7158 0798 6
Published by EP Publishing Limited, Bradford Road, East Ardsley, Wakefield, WF3 2JN, England

Cover photograph: Sporting Pictures (UK) Ltd
Translated by Ken Evans
Printed and bound in Great Britain by Butler & Tanner Ltd, Frome and London

Contents

It was with special satisfaction that I accepted the invitation to write a foreword to this book, since I feel that it will fill a large void in the bookcases of English-speaking cycling enthusiasts throughout the world. At long last we have a volume which covers every aspect of preparation for cycle racing, and in a manner which will leave the reader in no doubt as to the sound reasoning and experience upon which the advice is based.
Peter Konopka, whilst in contact with world class cyclists and coaches, gathered a tremendous fund of information. He then applied the analytical mind of the medic to the material and produced a training manual and reference book which should prove to be of untold value to the cycling reader. This book will be eagerly read by the aspiring racing cyclist, or coach, and I am certain that the riders and coaches from the upper echelons of the sport will be equally enthralled as the author examines the many facets of preparation for cycle racing.
The reader will find sections dealing with equipment, clothing, position on the bike, nutrition, training methods and programmes, and many other matters. In some instances, training principles which have been accepted for many years are given a thorough examination and many riders will, for the first time, really understand why they have been advised to adopt particular training methods. In other instances, the author introduces new principles and again ensures that the reader has a complete understanding of the reasons behind these new ideas. In both cases, I am certain that this understanding will encourage faith and commitment in training regimes which are laid down for this, the toughest sport in the world.
I commend this book to the reader, and hope that through the sound advice given by Peter Konopka, you will achieve maximum enjoyment from your participation in the sport of cycling, in the knowledge that you have performed in competition at the highest level possible in accordance with your physical ability.

Jim Hendry
Director of Racing and National Coach
British Cycling Federation

How this book came about

When, round about ten years ago, I was brought in to provide the medical back-up for the German national road-racing squad, I had no idea just how much cycle racing would enrich my life. I had, it is true, ridden a few races in my youth, but never had enough time to really get to know the secrets of cycle sport.

Since then these secrets have been revealed to me over years of fruitful collaboration with my friend Karl Ziegler, German national road and cyclo-cross coach; and this knowledge has been expanded by experience passed on to me by my boyhood hero, Rudi Altig, who shared with me many tales of his professional career. Last but not least, national coach Karl Link introduced me to track racing.

I have collaborated in the field of medical care of riders with Professor Armin Klümper. For me the call to become team doctor was a stimulus to renewed activity. I took up training again, raced in events for mature riders — and kept my eyes open! On my countless trips to world championships, Olympics, stage races and training camps, in Europe, North Africa and South America, I was able to gather a vast fund of knowledge, and for this I cannot sufficiently thank the BDR (German Cycling Federation). I became fascinated not only by the purely medical side of cycle sport, but by every other aspect of it as well: the secrets of pedal rhythms, questions of training programmes and diet, and even the equipment and the bikes themselves. I learned a great deal just by watching our experienced mechanic Manfred Otte, and later his successor Claus Lauer.

I believe I can be of considerable help to many cycle racing enthusiasts by sharing with them my own knowledge and that of acknowledged experts. For cycle sport, properly undertaken, can yield so much: it can make the body healthier, stronger, and younger. Anyone can cycle to keep fit, and even arthritis sufferers can continue to train for a long time on a bicycle, even when an ordinary stroll is no longer possible for them. Sportsmen of all types can begin their recovery from injury or operations at a very early stage with mobility training on a bike, thus safely satisfying the urge to get quickly back into training. Finally, winter sportsmen such as skiers, downhill or cross-country, and speed skaters, can fill in their summer 'off-season' period with cycle training.

In the course of writing everything down — above all in the technical sections — I soon found how hard it could be to set down in just the right words things which appeared quite clear to me. In this respect I have had much help from my friends Peter Krauss, coach of the RSG Augsburg, and from former professional rider Willi Singer. Also there at just the right moment, namely when I tackled the section on the history of cycle sport, was a man introduced to me by Karl Ziegler. His name is Wolfgang Gronen, and he enjoys the reputation of being a real databank of cycle sport. With Walter Lemke he has written a book on the history of the bicycle and cycle sport. He has given me many useful tips; from him came ideas and material for the 'Top Twelve', the line-up of the best dozen road and track riders of all time.

So this book grew out of my own experience, and that of other experts. I only hope that it introduces the reader to cycle sport sufficiently well to let him or her get as much out of it as I have.

Cycle sport — excitement and fascination

In recent years mankind has rediscovered the bicycle, despite the march of technology and the motor vehicle — or maybe because of it! Could it be that man, in trying to adapt himself to the age of technology, is finding his enforced lack of movement and exercise a real disadvantage? Fear of the diseases of civilization, and the desire for lasting good health, also play a part. Above all, there is a tendency in professional life to succumb to nervous tension and overwhelming pressures. These factors must bring about some kind of physical compromise. A form of endurance exercise can set man free from this kind of prison camp. It can improve the very quality of life.

My tip is to try cycle sport. Even today there are still many roads unspoiled by motor traffic — you only have to seek them out. Your cycle ride starts from your very door. You don't have to book in advance or queue up before you can participate. You can at least cycle when injury stops you going for a jog. And then there's the bonus of speed. Going flat out on a bike, you can match the swiftest racehorse — and all under your own steam!

But, speed apart, the fascination of cycle sport lies in the harmony between man and machine, between the sports apparatus and the 'human machine', the body itself. Whoever develops this harmony will follow cycle sport with a special passion that will never leave him.

In order to appreciate cycle sport to the full, therefore, you must get to know two things — the bicycle, and yourself. It is fascinating enough to find out how the bicycle developed, but there is more to knowing a bicycle than this. Once you have ridden your mount for a few thousand kilometres, taken it apart a few times and put it together again; once you have learned what makes it tick, recognized its strength and reliability; once you have learned what a precision instrument it is, then, and only then, can you really treasure it.

This book is intended to help awaken a love of cycling. Through cycling you find yourself in the best of company, for throughout the history of the bicycle famous discoverers, among the greatest minds of their time, artists, academics, barons and kings, have been gripped by the fascination of two wheels. As a reader you will learn how the modern precision racing bicycle is put together, and what you will need to know to enjoy cycle sport to the full. Included in this is the function of the human body, which has to be understood and appreciated. For cycling makes demands both physical and psychological, which the uninitiated may not appreciate. This book will show the cyclist how to get the best out of his sport, but that is not all. You will come to realize that your racing cycle is a helpful means to a long, healthy and efficient life.

Draisienne: a drawing from Baron Drais' patent application.

A short history of cycling and cycle sport

The wheel is one of mankind's greatest inventions, and all the greater because Nature offered the inventor no example to follow; no living organism has anything like a freely revolving wheel. The great advances of technology would have been impossible without the wheel, and surely history would have been radically different. The first wheels were of two- or three-part discs revolving about an axle. The oldest preserved representation of a waggon goes back to 3000 BC, and there have been suggestions of waggon wheels with spokes in Mesopotamian history around 2000 BC. Chinese records as far back as 4000 BC show a wheel with bevelled spokes.

For thousands of years the wheel was used only in conventional vehicles. No one had the notion of setting two wheels one behind the other and using the resulting vehicle to transport themselves. There was no reason they should have, for then there was no theory of the stabilising gyroscopic forces of revolving wheels.

The story of the bicycle really began in 1818, when Carl Friedrich Christian Ludwig Freiherr Drais von Sauerbronn patented his steerable hobbyhorse, later to be known as the 'Draisienne' in his honour. But simple forms of bicycles, wheels bound together with sticks, have been found in Egyptian and Chinese drawings from around 1300 BC. So for some 3000 years man had been busying himself with the thought that he could progress faster under his own steam.

In 1845 the mechanic Mylius constructed a bicycle whose front wheel was driven by cranks. A similar machine was made in 1853 by an instrument maker, Philipp Moritz Fischer. But it took a Frenchman, Pierre Michaux, to carry the design through to production, and in 1867, at the World Fair, he presented his *velocipede*, named the 'Michauline' after its inventor.

Since at first the front wheel was considered the driving wheel, it had to be made larger in order to cover more ground with one turn of the pedals. This accounted for

1869 racing machine (Michauline).

the development of the 'high bicycle', otherwise known as the Old Ordinary or Penny Farthing. For example, the Parisian mechanic Victor Renard built a high bicycle weighing 65kg, with a front wheel three metres in diameter! You can imagine what horrific crashes there were on bicycles of those dimensions. The first bicycle driven from the rear wheel was built by André Guilmet in 1868. Gradually the bicycle evolved from a wooden machine to an iron one, thanks to the tangential spokes of W. A. Cowper (1870), the rims of J. Truffauts (1875), and H. J. Lawson, who in 1879 placed the pedals between the wheels, so driving the rear wheel by chain. Solid rubber tyres, which had been used since 1869, were superseded in 1888 by the invention of pneumatic tyres, by veterinary surgeon John Boyd Dunlop.

One facet of man's nature is the wish to measure his strength against another's, and thus it was that, only two years after the invention of the hobby horse, there were races on them in Paris. In 1865 the first road race took place at Amiens, though it was only a 500m affair. The first international road race was in 1869, a distance event of 130km from Paris to Rouen. Even women took part! In 1880 a major event took place

B. Zierfuss, Berlin. German champion of 1893 with his Penny-Farthing.

over the Alps from Paris to Milan and back, and in the first modern Olympic Games (1896) there was an 87km road race. The first Tour de France took place in 1903. There were track races in England from 1868, and from 1882 in Germany, while the first six-day race took place in London in 1878, followed by the 1891 New York race and the Berlin six-day event of 1909.

The fascination of cycle sport went further than mechanics, engineers, technicians and watchmakers. Kaisers, Kings and other noblemen were woven into the fabric of its history. In 1868 Emperor Napoleon III struck a gold medal for a cycle race, and Kaiser Wilhelm I offered a superb trophy for a high-bicycle event; the Kaiser Trophy has been run annually ever since. The five Opel brothers distinguished themselves by taking successive victories in the Hessen championships, Ludwig von Opel even finishing runner-up in the world sprint championship in 1898 in Vienna.

The world of art had its cycling devotees too, such as Toulouse-Lautrec, Claude Monet, Pablo Picasso and Max Ernst, who all immortalized the bicycle on canvas, reflecting their preoccupation with it. Sir Edward Elgar was a dedicated cyclist. Other examples show what intelligent heads were turned by cycling. The Frenchman Albert Champion, who in 1899 won the first classic Paris-Roubaix behind motor pace, invented the sparking plug which still bears his name today. The brothers Orville and Wilbur Wright, pioneers of manned flight, raced on road and track, owned their own cycle business, and built their own machines. Cycle sport is studded with great names, such as Alfredo Binda, Costante Girardengo, Gino Bartali and Fausto Coppi. The Dortmund pairing of Kilian and Vopel dominated six-day racing for years. Some stars, such as Bartali, Ferdi Kubler, Louison Bobet, Jan Janssen, Jacques Anquetil, Daniel Morelon, Felice Gimondi and Eddy Merckx, have appeared on postage stamps, while streets, squares and stadiums have been named after others, such as Jean Robic, Guillermo Timoner, Victor Linart and Piet Moeskops.

But who were the greatest riders of all time? Obviously any selection is bound to be subjective, and it must take into account the difficulties of a period as well as a rider's successes. Some had it

G. P. Mills,
first winner of
the Bordeaux-Paris
race (1891).

easier than others, being the one top-class rider of their time instead of one star in a constellation of contemporaries.

Here, then, are the members of my exclusive club of 'all-time bests', in which only the most important names could hope for membership.

The twelve best road riders of all time

1. **Bartali,** Gino (Italy).
Born 18.7.1914.
Won the Giro d'Italia in 1936, 1937 and 1946, and the Tour de France in 1938 and 1948.

2. **Coppi,** Fausto (Italy).
Born 15.11.1918.
Died 2.1.1960 of malaria.
He was world pro road champion in 1952, won the Tour de France in 1949 and 1952, and the Giro d'Italia in 1940, 1947, 1949, 1952 and 1953.

3. **Kübler,** Ferdi (Switzerland).
Born 24.7.1919.
Won the Tour de Suisse in 1942, 1948, 1951, the Tour de France 1950, and was world pro road champion 1951.

4. **van Steenbergen,** Rik (Belgium).
Born 9.9.1924.
World pro road champion 1949, 1956, 1957.

5. **Bobet,** Louison (France).
Born 12.3.1925.
World pro road champion 1954. Tour de France winner 1953, 1954, 1955.

6. **Koblet,** Hugo (Switzerland).
Born 21.3.1925.
Died 6.11.1964 in car accident.
Winner Tour de Suisse 1950, 1953, 1955. Giro d'Italia 1950, Tour de France 1951.

7. **van Looy,** Rik (Belgium).
Born 20.12.1932.
World pro road champion 1960 and 1961.

8. **Anquetil,** Jacques (France).
Born 8.1.1934.
Tour de France winner 1957, 1961, 1962, 1963, 1964. Giro d'Italia 1960, 1964.

9. **Janssen,** Jan (Holland).
Born 19.5.1940.
World pro road champion 1964. Tour de France winner 1968.

10. **Gimondi,** Felice (Italy).
Born 29.9.1942.
World pro road champion 1973. Tour de France winner 1965, Giro d'Italia 1967, 1969, 1976.

11. **Merckx,** Eddy (Belgium).
Born 17.6.1945.
World amateur road champion 1964. World pro road champion 1967, 1971 and 1974. Tour de France winner 1969, 1970, 1971, 1972, 1974. Giro d'Italia winner 1968, 1970, 1972, 1973, 1974. Tour de Suisse 1974.

12. **Hinault,** Bernard (France).
Born 14.11.1954.
Tour de France winner 1978, 1979, 1981. World pro road champion 1980.

The twelve best track riders of all time

1. **Ellegaard,** Thorwald (Denmark).
Born 7.3.1877.
Died 22.4.1954.
Six times winner of the world pro sprint championship: 1901, 1902, 1903, 1906, 1908, 1911.

2. **Robl,** Thaddäus (Germany).
Born 22.10.1877.
Died 18.6.1910 (air crash).
Set up several world records on the tandem. In 1907 took five European motor-pace titles. World pro motor-paced champion 1901 and 1902.

3. **Meredith,** Leon (England).
Born 2.2.1883.
Died 2.2.1930 (ski accident).
Olympic champion in 1908, he was the only rider in history ever to win seven world amateur motor-paced titles (between 1904 and 1913).

4. **Linart,** Victor (Belgium).
Born 26.5.1889.
Died 15.10.1977.
World champion over 100km behind heavy motors 1921, 1924, 1926, 1927. World hour record-holder behind motors in 1921, with 86.280km.

5. **Moeskops,** Pieter Daniel (Holland).
Born 14.11.1893.
Died 15.11.1964.
Five times world pro sprint champion: 1921, 1922, 1923, 1924, 1926.

6. **Scherens,** Jef (Belgium).
Born 17.2.1909.
World pro sprint champion 1932, 1933, 1934, 1935, 1936, 1937, and 1947.

7. **Verschueren,** Dolf (Belgium).
Born 10.7.1922.
European pro motor-paced champion 1952, 1954, 1959 and 1961. World pro motor-paced champion 1952, 1953, 1954.

8. **Timoner,** Guillermo (Spain).
Born 24.3.1926.
Six times world pro motor-paced champion: 1955, 1959, 1960, 1962, 1964, 1965.

9. **Messina,** Guido (Italy).
Born 5.1.1931.
Olympic champion team pursuit 1952. World pro pursuit champion 1954, 1955, 1956. World amateur pursuit champion 1948 and 1953.

10. **Patterson,** Sid (Australia).
Born 14.8.1927.
World amateur sprint champion 1949. World amateur pursuit champion 1950. World pro pursuit champion 1952 and 1953.

11. **Maspes,** Antonio (Italy).
Born 14.1.1932.
Seven times world pro sprint champion: 1955, 1956, 1959, 1960, 1961, 1962, 1964.

12. **Morelon,** Daniel (France).
Born 24.7.1944
Seven times world amateur sprint champion: 1966, 1967, 1969, 1970, 1971, 1973, 1975. Gold medallist in the Olympics 1968 and 1972.

British international stars

The predominance of France, Italy, Belgium, Holland and Switzerland in cycle sport must be admitted, but Britain too has had its international stars.

Here are some of the best riders since the Second World War.

1. **Robinson**, Brian: A Yorkshireman from Mirfield who was the first Briton to win a Tour de France stage (at Brest in 1958), and who followed it up with another stage win in 1959. He lived in France as a semi-professional, and then as a full professional rider. He was the first British competitor to be accepted by the 'Continentals' as anything but a curiosity.

2. **Simpson**, Tom: Another Yorkshireman, who benefited from Robinson's guidance in his early years on the Continent where he was based in France, and later on in Belgium. He became the first Briton to wear the yellow jersey of race leadership in the Tour de France in 1962, and reached his peak when he won the world professional road championship in 1965. Other one-day classic victories were the 1961 Tour of Flanders, 1963 Bordeaux – Paris, 1964 Milan – San Remo and 1965 Tour of Lombardy. He died tragically during the thirteenth stage of the 1967 Tour de France, succumbing to the combined effects of heat, exertion on the climb up Mont Ventoux, and illegal stimulants, traces of which were found by a post-mortem.

3. A colleague of Simpson, who carried on where he left off, was Barry **Hoban**, once again a Yorkshire-based rider who moved to the Continent (first France, then Belgium). He won a total of eight Tour de France stages, a total unlikely to be equalled by any other Briton, and had one-day classic wins in Ghent-Wevelgem (1974) and the Henninger Turm (1966).

4. On the track, no one is remembered quite as much as Manchester's Reg **Harris**, who won the world amateur sprint title in 1947, and then the professional title in 1949, 1950, 1951 and 1954. 20 years later, at the age of 54, he made a brief comeback to take the British professional sprint title. He set several world records at the kilometre distance, and his track wins include 12 major Grand Prix.

5. More recently, Wolverhampton rider Hugh **Porter** set up a record in pursuit racing when he won his fourth world professional title in 1973, after previous triumphs in 1968, 1970 and 1972. He was also an excellent road rider, and won the season-long Star Trophy series in 1966 at a time when he had not even started to think about turning professional.

6. **Burton**, Beryl: She was never able to turn professional, but certainly reached the top of her sport. She was twice world women's road champion, in 1960 and 1967, and five times world pursuit champion, in 1959, 1960, 1962, 1963 and 1966. She has amassed more than 100 national titles on road and track, still breaking records at well over 40. Her peak was probably in 1967 when she broke the women's national 12-hour time trial record with more than 277 miles to her credit. In the same event the men's record fell too — at 276 miles.

Cycle sport today

Even in this age of technology and motorization, the bicycle is an appropriate piece of sporting apparatus. It combines sporting endurance exercise with the appeal of technology. A bicycle makes you independent of any energy crisis and offers health and well-being.

Lack of exercise is one of the reasons behind the growth of so-called 'civilized diseases'. The advantages of technology have been hard won in exchange for heart and circulatory disorders, breathing problems and obesity. Even in youth the problem is growing. The average physical capacity of schoolchildren and adolescents has clearly fallen. At least we should be able to set against the adverse effects of civilization the benefits of cycle sport, which exercises the whole body. And increasing leisure time makes some form of physical expression highly necessary. Certainly high-endurance sports such as running and cross-country skiing offer similar advantages. But not everyone is born to run, and there are many to whom running brings no pleasure at all. For this

A made-to-measure racing machine of a very expensive type. Frame and components are in titanium and titanium alloy. The future may bring new shapes and materials.

type of person the bicycle offers a pleasant way out. However, even top sportsmen like athletes and footballers may use cycling during enforced breaks through injury, and not lose much fitness as a result. After knee cartilage operations cycling can be begun before running is possible. Even the muscle wastage of the upper thigh after such operations can be minimized, or more quickly corrected. Cycling is also an effective method of summer training for all winter sports, especially cross-country and

Alpine skiing and speed skating. Especially today, cycling offers a number of advantages which really are worth considering.

Types of bicycle

Just as there are different types of cycling, so different types of bicycle have been developed. The types differ in a few essential details. The special demands of racing, varying from track events to cyclo-cross, dictate changes in the machines from tubing to tyres. But you can consider the sports bike such as young cyclists begin with as the basis for each type, and the sports machine has the advantage that you can also cycle to school on it!

The sports bike (semi-racer)

This machine has a very sporty look, and at first sight is very like a road-racing machine. Because of this similarity the 'sports' or semi-racer is the aim of every schoolboy, who finds it quite lightweight but nowhere near as expensive as a real racing bike.

A sports bike has mudguards, lights and a carrier which, although quite neat-looking, is businesslike enough to carry a schoolbag. Good sports bikes have 5, 10 or even 12-speed gears, two brakes, alloy cranks and double chainset, drop handlebars, a narrow saddle and 27in wheels with light tyres. The tyres are so-called 'wired-on' tyres, as opposed to tubular tyres, and can be easily mended if punctured. The sports bike is an easy-riding but still robust machine.

Road-racing machine.

The road-racing machine

A good road-racing machine is a precision work of art. Its frame is made out of specially light butted tubing, which gives it rigidity, manoeuvrability and light weight at the same time. The accessories are of expensive lightweight alloys such as dural and alloys of titanium: bottom bracket, cranks, chainwheels, pedals, handlebars and stem, gear mechanisms, hubs, spokes and rims, gear lever, brakes and brake levers, even toe-clips. The narrow racing saddle is usually plastic with a steel frame, padded

Aerodynamic road-racing machine. The frame and all the components (including the drinking bottle) were aerodynamically shaped by wind-tunnel testing.

Road-racing machine
with aluminium frame.

with foam and covered with leather. The slim tubular tyres are stuck on to the rims. The weight of such a machine would be between 8.5 and 10.5kg. But every bit of weight saved usually costs a lot more!

The track machine

The opposite of the road machine is the track bike. The frame is generally of a shorter design, the forks more upright, the fork blades not oval like a road bike but round, to cope with the increased lateral strains found in track events. The handlebar stem generally slopes steeply downwards, although some track riders prefer a flat extension. A track machine has no gear mechanism, brakes or freewheel. The rear wheel has a single fixed sprocket. The tyres weigh between 110 and 175g. Braking is simply by exerting backward pressure on the pedals, or by putting your gloved palm on the front tyre. The chainwheels and sprockets are usually thicker than on road machines. Chainwheels generally have between 47 and 53 teeth, with a rear sprocket having between 14

Track machine.

New type of track machine
under test by Daniel Gisiger.

and 16 teeth. The rear fork ends have horizontal openings ('track ends') and the hubs, unlike those on road machines, have no quick-release mechanism. The weight of a track machine is between 6 and 8kg.

The cyclo-cross machine

Basically similar to a road-racing machine, the bike used by a cyclo-cross rider has more clearance under the bottom bracket, more room below the fork crown, and the forks themselves are raked to a greater degree. The toe-clips are reinforced, and the gear-change lever is usually fixed into the end of the handlebar in place of the normal end plug, the advantage being that the rider can change gear without taking his hand from the bars. Gear changing is not quite so positive, however, because the cable is longer. Chainwheels have usually between 42 and 51 teeth, with a six-speed freewheel of 14 to 28 teeth. Brakes are a special centre-pull design, working upwards from below the rim braking surface. Normal brakes would be quickly clogged with mud and would soon seize up. The tyres weigh about 350g, and their treads vary in design depending on the course. A cyclo-cross bike weighs around

9kg, and lighter weights can only be achieved once again by the use of costly alloys for the accessories.

Handlebar control gear lever.

Special rim brakes for a cyclo-cross bike.

Cross tyre with studded tread.

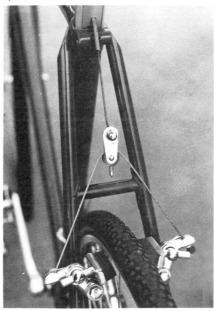

The 'stayer bike' for motor-paced racing

Stayer races are run off behind pacing motorcycles, and so, to minimise the distance between the rider and pacer, this kind of machine has a smaller front wheel (24in), the head tube is upright, and the forks are reversed. The handlebars are deeper, and on the end of a much longer extension, which in turn is linked for support with the fork crown. The saddle too has extra support in the form of a rod from the top tube to its nose, and the saddle itself is shorter. Stayer races are usually run off at between 60 and 80kph, and some open-air events have produced speeds of 115kph! The special tubular tyres are further attached to the rims by special bandages, so that even in the event of a puncture they will not roll off the rim and cause potentially fatal crashes. Stayer bikes have no brakes, gear-change or freewheel, but instead have a single fixed sprocket. The chainwheel usually has 66 teeth, with a sprocket of 14 or 15 teeth depending on the track. Weight is about 7.5kg. The pacing motorcycles have no gearbox or clutch, and are usually powered by a 1000cc

two-cylinder engine of some 10hp. The pacer races standing up in stirrups at the level of the rear axle, in order to give his rider maximum shelter. The handlebars are swept back, the grips being at the level of the pacer's hips.

Artistic cycling: Manfred Maute,
world champion 1968, 1971
and 1972.

Two-man cycle ball.

Stayer race: in the foreground pacemaker
Stakenburg with Horst Schutz; in the
background, pacemaker Durst with
Wilfried Peffgen.

Derny-paced race: as with stayer races, the
rider races in the slipstream of a motorcycle,
but this is a special Derny machine, ridden
by Francesco Moser.

Indoor cycling

The cycle-ball machine
This is of very special construction,
with upturned handlebars, small
wheels, a fixed wheel and very low
gearing. As with a track machine,
there are no brakes, and slowing
down is by backward pressure.
Such a bike weighs about 13kg.
This facet of the sport can be
practised indoors (as cycle-ball) or
outdoors (as cycle-polo).

The artistic cycling machine
These machines have special
gearing to allow the rider to
perform unusual manoeuvres and
acrobatics. The emphasis is on
artistic performance, achieved on a
machine in motion. These bikes
have upturned bars, small wheels,
fixed sprocket and 1:1 gearing. The
forks are vertical and the saddle is
specially shaped, with an upswept
rear section.

The individual machine

The essence of cycle sport is in the interplay of man and machine. For this reason, the two elements must be completely suited. Every racing cyclist should have his own machine designed specially for his own physique, and for the kind of cycling to be tackled. One centimetre more or less on the frame size can greatly influence how efficiently the bicycle can be ridden. Frame height and saddle position must be individually tailored to the shape and size of the athlete concerned. Only thus can the best and most efficient riding style be obtained, and the greatest physical output be achieved.

The bicycle frame must not only be tailored specially to suit the rider's own build, but it must also have certain intrinsic properties. It must be strong and rigid, yet at the same time light and manoeuvrable. The strength of the rider must be passed on to the transmission system without undue wastage. In motion, there are pulling, bending and twisting strains applied to the frame, in relation to the rider's body weight. On the saddle, these strains can work out to $1\frac{1}{2}$ times body weight; pedals undergo some $1\frac{3}{4}$ times body weight, and the handlebars twice body weight.

Yet even though a racing machine must undergo all these strains, it should not weigh more than 9 to 11kg (for a road machine) or 6.5 to 8kg (track machine). It is reckoned that every extra kilogram on the fixed (i.e. non-revolving) part of the bicycle — such as the frame — requires an extra energy output of between 1 and 2 per cent, at a speed of 35 to 42kph. This percentage increases on uphill efforts, or at higher speeds. On the other hand, a bicycle that is too light has no advantage, for the frame could be weak, and 'whip' too much, thus causing expensive energy loss. For this reason it is important to select the components of an individualized racing cycle most carefully. Taller riders need a larger frame which is made stiffer and thus heavier, so it will not 'whip'. Smaller riders can use a lighter frame without problems. But it is always necessary that the key parts of the bicycle, such as gear mechanisms, brakes and so on should be of top quality.

The road-racing bicycle is composed of:

1. The frame.
2. The steering assembly: handlebars, headset and forks.
3. The transmission: bottom bracket, cranks, chainwheels, pedals, toe-clips and straps, freewheel block and chain.
4. The wheels: hubs, rims, spokes and tyres.
5. The saddle and seat pillar.
6. The brakes and brake levers.
7. The gearing, with front changer and rear mechanism plus control levers.
8. The accessories, such as pump, spare tyre, bottle and bottle-cage, even a cyclometer.

The components of a road-racing bicycle

These days it's not so difficult to buy a road bike. There is a real multiplicity of models on offer, and the choice can leave the layman speechless. Modern racing cycles are masterpieces, and are priced accordingly. A good racing bike can cost between £300 and £600. You can buy one cheaper, but you can also pay even more. Prices of more than a thousand pounds are possible for real 'specials' that are generally built around a titanium alloy frame, which makes them very light but still strong enough for the job. Still, even professionals don't use such machines for normal road racing, reserving them for time trials and similar special events. To sum up, you don't have to get the most expensive and lightest bicycle; you can find one which offers a compromise between lightness and stability. With cheap bicycles, money is saved on the quality of components such as brakes, gears, bottom bracket and headset. These parts are better replaced later by others which are race-proven, reliable and hard-wearing. But why are racing cycles so expensive?

Apart from the fact that a racing machine is a complete piece of sporting apparatus, it is made up of so many pieces that are precision-made, complex and for the most part hand-finished, that the price is bound to reflect this. The connoisseur just selects his frame and equipment and does not ask the price.

Not only so as to hand-pick the parts, but also for his own peace of mind, the buyer of a racing machine should know each component, how to look after it properly, and thus have many years of enjoyment from the bike.

The frame

The frame is the most important part of the racing bicycle, and consists of the following parts:

1. Top tube
2. Seat tube
3. Down tube
4. Head tube
5. Bottom bracket shell
6. Rear triangle
7. Forks
8. Drop-outs

The frame is made up normally of round main tubes and tapering forks, seat stays and chain stays, the main tubes being made from metal 0.7 – 1.0mm thick. The frame material is usually of a chrome-molybdenum alloy steel. Weight is saved on the main tubes by a process called butting, which means the tubes are thinned out internally where less strength is needed. The tubing has to be put together so that the finished frame can withstand static and dynamic loads. Most popular tubing is the English Reynolds or the Italian Columbus, which is usually jointed with lugs, and hand-finished. The best frames are all hand-made, and generally weigh around 2.5kg.

There are also some extremely light aluminium frames, whose tubes are screwed together and then glued. But they are frequently not rigid enough, and may not be strong enough to support a heavy rider. This weakness in the frame is translated into a loss of energy by the time the rider's efforts reach the transmission, a disadvantage which is shared by titanium-alloy and other ultra-light frames.

Generally speaking, large frames are less rigid than small

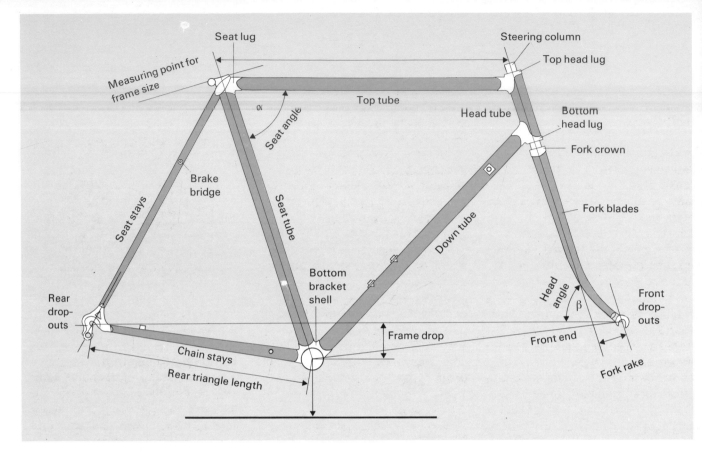

Seat lug

Measuring point for frame size

Steering column

Top head lug

α Seat angle

Top tube

Head tube

Bottom head lug

Fork crown

Brake bridge

Seat stays

Seat tube

Down tube

Fork blades

Rear drop-outs

Bottom bracket shell

Head angle

β

Front drop-outs

Chain stays

Frame drop

Front end

Rear triangle length

Fork rake

frames, the effect being exaggerated at moments of extreme stress, or during steep descents. Too light a bike with a weak frame can become difficult to handle on a descent, and may give rise to a feeling of 'fluttering'. Thus bigger riders must go for a stiffer and consequently heavier frame, while lighter-built riders can use relatively light frame

tubing. Also, a frame can suffer from metal fatigue when it is worn out after covering too many kilometres or rough surfaces. The molecules loosen up, and the frame becomes 'soft'. For this reason from time to time the frame has to be changed — although the time interval differs — while the other components of the bicycle can continue in use.

The relationship between height and frame size:

Height	Frame size
160–165cm	51–53cm
165–170cm	53–55cm
170–175cm	55–57cm
175–180cm	57–58cm
180–185cm	58–59cm
185cm plus	59–60cm

Frame size

The best equipment in the world is useless if the frame is the wrong size for the individual's body and build. The critical measurement for the frame is its basic size measured from the centre of the bottom bracket shell to the top of the seat lug. You can either work out your frame size from your height (see table opposite) or from your inside leg measurement (see illustration). In case of doubt, go for a frame slightly too small, rather than too large.

If you differ from the average build — for instance, if you have very

Relationship between leg length and frame size. The leg length corresponds to the distance from saddle top to the pedal at its lowest point. If you deduct 25cm, then you have approximately the correct frame size.

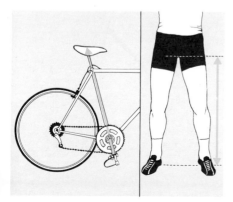

short or very long arms, a very long or very short upper body — then you will need to go to a specialist for a made-to-measure frame. Such a frame will take into account any physical peculiarities, although there is always some possibility of adjustment through using a longer or shorter handlebar stem. Young riders who are still growing should take this into account and select a frame on the large side.

Riders under 1.60m should buy a frame of 50cm or less. Taller riders refer to the table. You can adjust your position by moving the saddle and the handlebar assembly.

Drop-outs

The drop-outs — front and rear fork ends — accept the wheels. The rear right-hand drop-out almost always has a hanger, to which the gear mechanism is bolted. The correct placing of the drop-outs is important for the stability, safety and perfect functioning of the bicycle.

Steering system

This consists of:
1. The handlebars and extension (stem)

Drop-outs (fronts above, rear below).

2. The headset
3. The forks

Handlebars and stem

You should think of the handlebars and stem as an entity. The stem is fixed into the fork column by means of an expander bolt. This handlebar assembly can be split into three distinctive components: the handlebar bend itself, the stem, and the expander bolt.

Handlebar and stem.

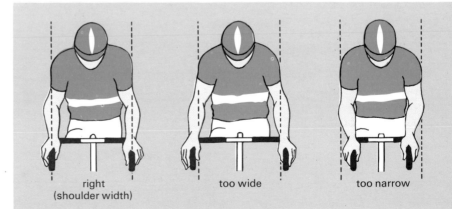

Handlebars of various shapes.
1. Road bar (*Tour de France* or *Giro d'Italia* type).
2. Rounded form of track or road bar (*Gimondi* or *Anquetil* type).
3. Track bar, deep bend.

Handlebars

The tube forming the handlebar is usually made of duralumin, 1mm thick and between 23 and 25mm outside diameter. We generally measure the width of handlebars at the two ends, from centre to centre, and this width should correspond to the width of the rider's shoulders (see illustration). Too narrow a handlebar, and the breathing is restricted; too wide, and the arm muscles quickly become fatigued. Be careful, though; some Italian bars are measured outside to outside, and so would give a measurement about a centimetre greater. A 40cm width will suit the majority of riders. Broader and slimmer riders must select their bars accordingly.

There is quite a choice of handlebar shapes (see illustration). Most road machines are fitted with a *Tour de France* or *Giro d'Italia* type, both models offering three comfortable gripping positions: on the top part of the bars, over the brake-lever hoods, and on the dropped part. The ends of the bars must be plugged with end stops, to avoid risk of injury in crashes. This is such an important point that it has been made an international regulation. The bars are covered with tape, so that a better grip is ensured, neither slippery when wet, nor sticky in the heat. There are even special leather sleeves nowadays.

Handlebar width (cm)	Frame size (cm)	Type of rider
36–38	Up to 51	Children
38–39	51–55	Small riders
39–40	56–58	Normal size
40–41 and over	59 and larger	Very broad riders

Put more simply, slimly built riders should go for 38cm, normal build 40cm, and broad, powerful riders for 42cm.

right
(shoulder width)   too wide   too narrow

Stem or extension

The handlebars are held firmly in the extension by a clamp bolt. The extension, usually in duralumin, slopes down at an angle which varies, depending on the rider's build and the type of cycling (see illustration). The 'Sprint' pattern slopes more steeply downwards, and allows the sprinter to assume a much more arched position. Two less steeply sloping types of extension cater for road racing.

The length of the forward extension is related to the size of the frame, and the rider's build. It is worked out in these proportions:

Length	Frame size
8– 9cm	51–53cm
9–10cm	53–55cm
10–11cm	55–57cm
11–12cm	57–59cm
12–13cm	59–60cm

The handlebars should be fixed in the stem so that the lower part is either horizontal or slightly inclined downwards. Changing the length of the extension enables a rider to cater for his physical peculiarities, such as very short or very long arms.

The expander

The name refers to the component which fixes the stem tightly into the fork column. By tightening the bolt at the top of the stem, a conical nut is drawn up into its shaft, tightening it against the inner surface of the fork column.

The headset

The headset fixes the fork column within the head tube, and consists of bearings at the top and bottom of the head tube, a locking washer, and a locknut, the bearings themselves being of special quality. Headsets can be made from steel, duralumin or titanium, the last two saving weight but clearly at a price. Just how long a headset lasts depends on two aspects: the quality of the components, and how well they are fitted. Properly adjusted, a headset should have virtually no play, yet the bars and stem should still be able to turn quite freely. Too loosely adjusted, the bearings and races can quickly become damaged. Set too tightly, they can become pitted, and also give the rider a very upsetting feeling. Fitting a headset is very important. It is a matter of a special touch,

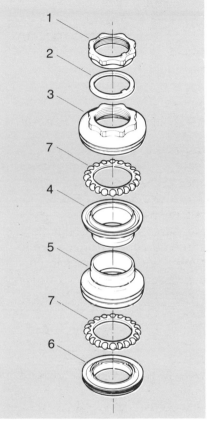

Headset, made of the following parts: 1. Locknut; 2. Lock washer; 3. Screwed race; 4. Top head race; 5. Bottom head race; 6. Crown race; 7. Caged bearings.

and should be entrusted to an expert.

29

The forks

The forks are in effect components of the frame, and usually of the same colour, although chrome-plating has become very popular. But, functionally speaking, the forks are really a part of the steering system. The forks are made up of the fork column, in which the stem is fitted with the expander bolt; the fork crown, on which

Forks, made up of fork column, fork blades and front drop-outs.

rests the crown race of the headset; the curved fork-blades; and the drop-outs. The fork crown must be precisely constructed, so that it fits the crown race of the headset. The life of the headset will be considerably shortened if this is not so. The handling of the bicycle depends to a great extent on the angle of the head tube (the head angle) and on the rake of the forks. Forks for road bikes have a rake of about 5cm. More upright forks mean less loss of energy when the rider gets 'out of the saddle', such as in mountain events or races with a lot of climbs. But very upright forks are only for extremely good road surfaces. The cross-section of the fork blades is oval, in order to better absorb the shocks of uneven surfaces.

The transmission system

The strength of the rider's legs is passed on to the pedals, fitted with toe-clips and straps. It then passes to the cranks, a lever system acting about the bottom bracket axle. The right crank is attached by arms (usually five) to the chainring or rings, on which runs the chain that transmits the power to the freewheel sprockets, and thence to the rear hub, spokes, rims and tyres.

Pedals, toe-clips and straps

Racing pedals are usually made of duralumin. Different makes, such as Campagnolo, Shimano, Sun Tour, Maillard, Zeus or Lyotard, have varying weights and prices. The lightest pedals are the Campagnolo Super Record, with titanium axles. Campagnolo's steel pedals are heavier, but they wear well and can last the life of a bicycle.

Toe-clips

Toe-clips come in short, medium and long versions. The length, measured from the middle of the pedal-axle to the front of the clip, relates to the rider's shoe size (see table). You can vary the length of clips slightly by

Pedal with toe-clips and straps.

inserting some washers against the fixing bolts, but remember that there should always be a gap of some 2mm between the front of the shoe and the clip itself. A

Aerodynamic pedal (Shimano DD design). The axle is higher, and the toe-clip can be adjusted both for length and horizontal position.

protection for the shoe could be a few turns of handlebar tape around the front of the clip.

Relationship between shoe size and toe-clip length:

Shoe size	Toe-clip type	Length
37, 38, 39	Short clips	7.5cm
40, 41, 42	Medium clips	8.5cm
43, 44, 45, and 46	Long clips	9.5cm

Straps
Toe-straps are around 38cm long and 1cm wide, the end coming to a point. The other end is fitted with a quick-release buckle, which can be rapidly loosened with a flick of the hand or thumb, but which will not come loose of its own accord. This buckle should be placed directly above the pedal, so that there is no friction on the outside of the foot. The toe-strap end can be bound with tape to give a better grip for the fingers.

The chainset
The bottom bracket is fixed in the bottom bracket housing with two cups and ball-bearings or ball-races. The bottom bracket, cranks and chainwheels are

usually of duralumin. Some axles are even of titanium, consequently lower in weight but higher in price. It is essential that the bottom bracket set, the cranks and chainwheels (also called chainrings) should fit perfectly, and so they are usually from the same manufacturer. The best-known makes are Campagnolo, Shimano, Sun Tour, Sugino, Zeus and Stronglight. The bottom bracket should be adjusted so that there is no sideways play, yet so that the axle still turns freely. Nowadays bracket sets either have a liner, or are watertight units, so that during wet races no rain can get in. The cranks fasten to each end of the axle, the right-hand crank having five arms to which the chainwheels are bolted. The crank length, measured from the centre of the bracket axle to the centre of the pedal axle, will vary depending on the rider's leg length.

☐ Riders of average build, using a frame of 56 to 59cm, should use cranks of 170 to 172.5mm.

☐ Smaller riders, frame size 50 to 55cm, are best to stick to 170mm.

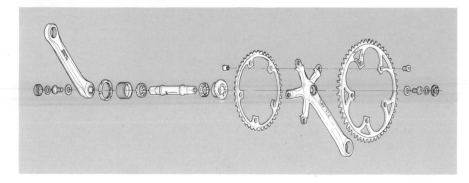

Chainset, with cranks and chainwheels, exploded view.

☐ Tall riders, on frames of 60 to 61cm, should use 175mm cranks.

Most professionals choose 172.5mm, but when greater leverage is required, such as on mountain time trials, they go for 175 or even 180mm. On the other hand, on short circuit races, where it helps to pedal through tight corners, they will use 170mm.

As cranks get longer, leverage increases, but of course the foot travels a greater distance on each pedal stroke, making fast pedalling more difficult. With short cranks, the opposite is the case, so each rider should choose a crank length which relates to his build, the type of racing, and the type of pedalling required, going for the right compromise between leverage and fast pedalling.

The five arms of the right-hand crank are bolted to the chainrings (usually two of them), a larger outer ring and a smaller inner.

Generally, chainrings have between 41 and 54 teeth, and a typical choice for average conditions would be a 42 inner and 53 outer.

The chain

The chain is moved across from one chainwheel to another by the front changer. On a road machine the chain is narrow ($1/2 \times 3/32$in; 13×2.4mm) and has around 108 links, held together by rivets. The 'spring link' used to join the chain on ordinary bicycles is not used on racing machines, because it would foul the freewheel or the rear mechanism.

The chain must be the right length, so that when it is on the large chainwheel and the middle-sized freewheel sprockets, it runs freely without being under any strong tension. When the chain is on the small chainwheel and the smallest sprockets, it should run without drooping.

The chain line

The chain line should be parallel to the middle line of the frame (see illustration). It runs from the middle point between the two chainrings to the middle of the freewheel block — on the third sprocket of a five-speed, and between the two centre sprockets on a six-speed. Small variations from this ideal can be corrected by the use of hub spacing washers.

If a chain is too far out of line, there is much energy lost through friction; it is important, therefore, to adjust your combinations of front chainring and rear sprockets so that the chain stays as straight as possible. This is explained in detail later.

The freewheel

The freewheel (or 'block') is normally screwed to the rear hub, although there are unit hubs which include a freewheel body. Every freewheel consists of a body and sprockets of several sizes. Mostly these blocks are of steel, but there are also lighter (and more expensive) models which use duralumin or titanium. The number of teeth on the sprockets can be changed. There are blocks with five, six or seven sprockets, but the most typical is a six-speed of 13, 14, 15, 17, 19 and 21 teeth. If you arc putting on a five-speed, then the best solution would be to leave off the 13, for this sprocket should only be used by highly-trained riders. In special terrain, such as mountain events, sprockets as low as 26 or 28 teeth can be used. Recently the 12-tooth sprocket has been introduced, but its use is really limited to top riders in time trials, or on mountain descents.

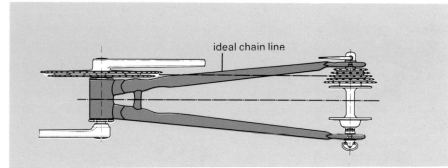

Chain line: the ideal chain line lies parallel to the centre line of the frame.

Freewheel, exploded view. 1, 2 and 3, sprockets; 4. washers; 5. freewheel body.

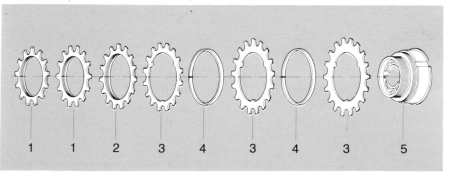

Freewheels: Regina model (right), Shimano (left).

Handling big gears is a skill which has to be learned, and beginners should not attempt it, for they will lose all their pedalling skill and rhythm if they do. For this reason there are widespread regulations against the use of big gears by young riders. Anyone buying a machine for schoolboy or junior racing should make sure that the gear ratios are within the rules of the cycling governing body.

Sprint wheels

These are special wheels for racing, and consist of rims, spokes, hubs and tyres. A racing wheel should be built so it runs smoothly and is perfectly round and true. Every spoke should have equal tension, so that they

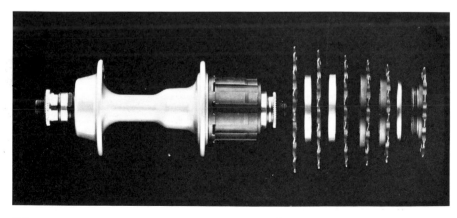

Cassette freewheel and hub.

share equally the shocks of riding. Any that are overtight may break. Newly-built wheels should not be used for a race, because they need to settle in; the spoke nipples must bed down properly. Usually an energetic training run of 100km should be enough to achieve this, after which the wheels should be tightened and trued again. Normal spoking for road-racing is 36, but 40, 32, 28 and 24 spokes are also used. Spoking of less than 36 has the advantage of lowered weight and less wind resistance, but such wheels are more prone to damage than 36-spoked versions. If just one spoke breaks, the rim can buckle badly, making further progress impossible. For this reason you should be absolutely sure that your need to use 32 spokes or less is really worth the risk of having to give up the race because of spoke breakage, or at the very least, of having to turn to the service car for a spare. For road racing 36 spokes are generally best. Road-racing wheels are normally built 'crossing three' or 'crossing four'. This means that two spokes which cross near the hub are four spoke-holes apart at the rim (crossing three) or six (crossing

Wheel components ready for assembly: rim, hub, spokes and nipples.

Ready-spoked and trued wheel, 36 spokes.

four). Wheels built crossing four are not so stiff, but tend to last longer.

Rims

Normal rims for road racing are up to 22mm wide, and weigh between 300 and 450g each. There are many different models and manufacturers (such as Mavic, Fiamme, Weinmann, Super Champion, Nisi). The lightest rim is probably the Nisi Special, which is 19mm wide and weighs only 200g. On the grounds of stability, heavy riders should not choose very light or narrow rims.

Spokes

At their thicker ends, spokes for racing bicycles usually measure between 1.8 and 2mm in diameter. These so-called 'double-butted' spokes are either stainless steel, or chrome-plated. Building and truing a wheel is both a science and an art which only a few experts really master. Each spoke should have the same tension as the next one, and the rim should be perfectly true. For this you need a wheel-building stand and a lot of experience. As well as normal round spokes, flattened ones, which cut down wind resistance, are also available. Don't forget to 'bed in' the spokes of a newly-built wheel on a training ride — never in a race!

Hubs

Enormous forces work on the hubs of a racing wheel, so here is no place to skimp. Experienced racing cyclists choose their hubs from among the top ranges, such as Campagnolo Record, Shimano Dura-Ace, Zeus 2000, Maillard 700 or Sun Tour Superbe. Most manufacturers also offer a cheaper range, so watch what you are buying.

Large-flange hubs.

Small-flange hubs.

Hubs have either large or small flanges, the flange being the area around the hub barrel to which the spokes are attached. Small-flange hubs are lighter and cheaper, and are good for use in training and most races. Large-flange hubs take a shorter spoke, and therefore the wheels built with them are stronger and stiffer, good for use in circuit races and in mountain events, especially with 32 spokes or fewer.

Buying cheaper hubs can work out

Shimano Dura-Ace cassette hubs.

dearer in the end. They are generally of cheaper raw material, the spoke holes are often not as true and, above all, not countersunk. This puts extra stresses on the spokes at the flange, and thus they are more prone to breakage, which can damage rims too. Broken spokes should be replaced only by an expert, and the wheels trued again.

Sturmey-Archer Dynohub, used to power lighting on dark training runs.

Quick-release

Racing hubs are equipped with quick-release mechanisms, which make for more rapid wheel-changes during a race. A flick of the lever either tightens or loosens the hub in the drop-outs.

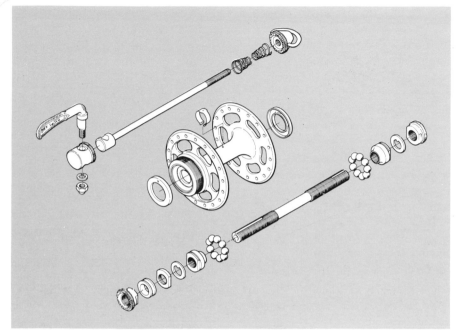

Hub and quick-release skewer, exploded view.

Clement Elvezia 75, 330g.
Use: Training.

Continental Wooden track, 180g.
Use: Track.

Wolber Renforce, 430g.
Use: Touring or lightweight cyclo-cross.

Wolber Cross Super, 420g.
Use: Cyclo-cross in heavy going.

Tyres

Racing wheels always have special tyres called 'tubulars', which are constructed with a carcass of fine cotton or silk, joined underneath by stitching. This stitching is in turn protected by a chafing tape. Inside the carcass is sewn an extra-light inner tube. On the outer surface of the carcass is stuck or vulcanised a light tread, which can weigh as little as 20g on a track tyre, or 80g for a heavy road tyre. The best tyres are hand-finished, and because the market is small, they always tend to be in short supply.

Generally speaking, the lighter a tubular is, the more expensive it will be. Dearest of all are the silk tyres such as the Clement Criterium Seta Extra, which weighs only 185g. Such tyres are used normally for events on very good surfaces. There are track

Clement Criterium, 240g.
Use: Road races.

Vittoria Corsa CX, 230g.
Use: Road races.

Continental type 220, 240g.
Use: Road races.

tyres which weigh only 100g, but a typical road tyre will weigh 220–240g. In training, you can use tyres of 260 to 300g, yet this is still considerably lighter than a touring tyre and tube, which weigh 800 to 1100g! Tubular tyres give better performance if 'matured'. Tyres which come straight from the factory are more prone to

punctures. The maturing process hardens the tread and reduces the puncture risk. For this reason, buy your tyres in advance, and keep them one to three seasons in a cool, dark, dry room, best of all lightly inflated on old rims. Never start a race with untried tyres. Always give them a reasonable test ride, so that you won't be let down unexpectedly. Tubulars are kept on the rim either by special rim tape or by tubular cement. Before mounting a new tyre, the rim should be coated several times with cement, so as to build up a good 'bed'. The tyre should also be stretched a little before it goes on to the rim.
Tubulars have special high-pressure valves. You unscrew the lock-nut first, press the stem slightly to check that air can escape, then release and connect the pump.

Tyre pressure
The recommended tyre pressure depends on the type of tyre and the weight of the rider. Silk tyres for track racing or road time trials can easily be pumped up to 8 or 9 atmospheres, or even more; normal cotton tubulars are better with 6 or 7. Top-quality road

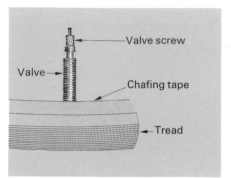

Tubular tyre valve. This is called a Presta valve. Before pumping the air in, the valve must first be unscrewed.

tubulars such as the 240g Continental or the 195g Clement Criterium can take 8 atmospheres or more. One point to watch, however, is that tyres aren't pumped so hard that they lose adhesion on the corners, especially in the wet. On the other hand, tyres at too low a pressure have more drag, and consequent loss of energy. The important thing is to get the right pressure for the occasion, and for this purpose a 'track pump' — a two-handed pump with a gauge — is invaluable.
If you don't have a track pump with a gauge, there is a simple test. If you press hard on the tread with your thumbs, it should

give, but never so much that you can feel the rim surface.
After each ride, let out some of the air. This prolongs the tubular's effective life.

Spare tyre

In every race and on every training ride you should carry a spare tubular, either strapped underneath the saddle, in the bottle cage, or in the back pocket of your jersey. Longer training runs mean it's sensible to take two spares. Best used as spares are older tyres which have already been ridden. Firstly, it is quicker to fit them, because unlike a new tyre they don't have to be stretched to fit on to the rim. And secondly, they will be safer, because old rim cement still on the tyre will blend with any residue on the rim to form a workable bond. New tyres, without glue, could easily roll off and cause an accident.
Spare tyres should be folded carefully, in fact virtually rolled up. Starting at the fold opposite the valve, the tyre should be folded over and over on itself, pushing any air left in the tyre up towards the valve, which can then be released, and the air let out. In this way the tyre takes up

Choosing tyre pressures

Type of event	Carcass	Weight (g)	Pressure (atmospheres)
Track			
Sprint or record attempts	Silk	100–110	10–11
Most events	Silk	120–140	9–10
Motor-paced	Cotton	180–220	9–10
Tandem	Cotton	280–300	9–10
Road			
Training	Cotton	350–380	6–7
Good road races	Cotton	180–230	8–9
Bad surfaces	Cotton	280–300	7–8
Cyclo-cross	Cotton	300–320	6–7

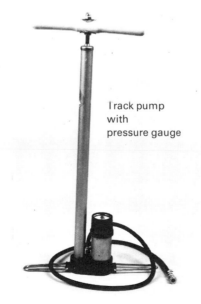

Track pump with pressure gauge

the least amount of room. The folded tyre is then rolled up inside a plastic bag, so that it doesn't get wet. It's advisable from time to time to unfold the spare and

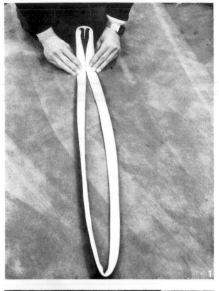

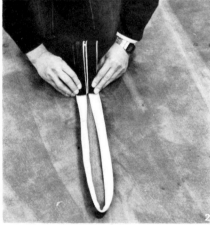

This is how you fold up a spare tyre, so that it takes up as little room as possible and the valve does not chafe the tyre.

pump it up, to test whether it still holds air. Sometimes a badly folded or unprotected tyre can puncture through rubbing against the edge of the saddle.

One more tip. If you have to ride through road works or over rough surfaces, place your palm (wearing a track mitt, of course!) lightly against the tread of the tyres, which will scrape off any sharp material which could cause punctures either immediately or later, after working their way gradually through the tread rubber. This manoeuvre is carried out on the move, so be careful to keep your fingers out of the spokes! You will see experienced riders doing this automatically, without taking their attention from the road.

Seat pillars and saddles

The seat pillar (also known as a seat post or saddle pillar) must be a good fit into the seat tube, usually secured by an allen-key bolt. Not for the racing man the ordinary seat pillar with a separate saddle clip. These are too heavy and difficult to adjust. Instead, a special seat pillar with an adjustable cradle, such as the Campagnolo, TTT, Simplex, SR and so on. It is very important to be able to get the saddle height just right. For safety's sake, the seat pillar should extend at least 6cm into the seat tube, but remember that anything more than this means excess weight to be carried.

The saddle is a very important piece of equipment — as the budding cyclist will very soon discover! From the beginning, you have to get used to the comparatively hard 'feel' of a racing saddle.

Originally, only leather saddles were used for racing. These are relatively hard, yet soften gradually and fit themselves to the rider's anatomy. The tension of such a saddle can be adjusted by tightening the nose bolt. But preparing a leather saddle is a job

Saddle with saddle pillar.

for an expert, and once it has been nicely softened and shaped, it still has to be carefully treated after each rainy outing, otherwise it will buckle and the leather lose its suppleness. Another disadvantage is the weight (around 600g). Yet top-quality leather saddles, such as Brooks, are still used today.

Most riders today use plastic saddles, which are lightly padded with plastic foam, then covered with suede or smooth leather. They are light in weight (about 350g), need no 'breaking in', and do not need special care in bad weather. Saddles without padding, but with a simple smooth

leather covering, are cheaper, but on them you tend to slide about. Suede or buffalo leather gives a better grip; buffalo is probably best because it wears longer. The saddle is another place not to skimp, so buy the best you can afford.

Brakes and brake levers

Brakes have either side-pull or centre-pull mechanisms. Side-pull brakes have fewer components, and are therefore lighter. But because the cable pulls on one side of the brake they tend to need centring more often. Centre-pull brakes hardly ever need this extra attention. Their braking pull is more even, but not as powerful. Because of the advantage of the side-pull in actual braking power, the majority of professionals prefer them. The most widely used

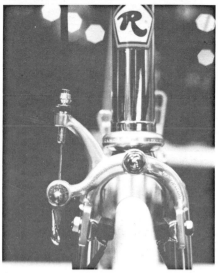

Campagnolo rim brake.

top-quality brake comes from Campagnolo. Their brakes are dear, but in performance they are unsurpassed. Apart from Campagnolo, other racing brakes come from Mafac, Shimano,

Centre-pull brake (not often used).

Superlight saddles with aluminium frames (Cinelli) weighing only 200g.

Brake levers.

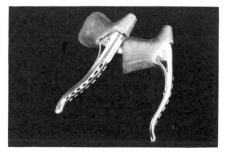

Detail of a time trial machine (Colnago Gold, 7.8kg) with front brake mounted behind the fork crown.

Weinmann, Zeus and so on. Good brakes have some form of quick-release system, either on the brake lever or on the stirrup. Such a system increases the distance between the brake blocks. Primarily this is to allow a quicker wheel-change, but a supplementary advantage is that when a spoke breaks and the wheel buckles, you can continue without the rim rubbing against the brake-blocks at every revolution.

The brake levers should be fixed to the handlebars in such a position that it's easy to operate them either from the top or when

CB rim brake, smallest in the world.

your hands are on the dropped part of the bars. When the brakes are full on, there should be no danger of the lever pulling right back to touch the handlebars. It is important to adjust the brake blocks so that when you brake they work directly on the rim itself, and do not touch the tyre. Another important point is to cover the end of the cable with a cap, to stop it fraying out. Most brake shoes are open at one end, and they should be fitted so that the friction with the rim tends to force the block against the closed end — not the open one! (See illustration.)

The right way to fit brake shoes, so that the closed end of the shoe is in the direction of travel.

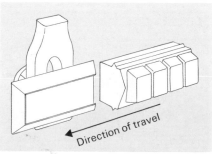

Direction of travel

Gear mechanisms

These consist of the front changer, acting on the double chainwheel, the rear mechanism, the gear cables, and the control levers. The front changer moves the chain from large to small chainwheel and vice versa. The rear mechanism moves it from sprocket to sprocket on the freewheel. This way, if you have two chainwheels and six freewheel sprockets, you have a theoretical choice of twelve gear ratios. But because of bad chain alignment, you generally lose at least two of them (see illustration). If the chain is on the biggest chainring, then you would not use the largest freewheel sprocket, for the chain would then be too far out of line and would create too much friction on the freewheel sprocket teeth. For a similar reason, you wouldn't use the small chainring with the smallest sprocket. Taking these two lost ratios into account, you should work out a series of chainwheel and sprocket variations which give as many different choices of ratio as possible. For this a gear table will help (see page 88) or you can use the previously suggested combinations of 53/42 rings

Chain lines should be kept as straight as possible, otherwise there are friction losses.

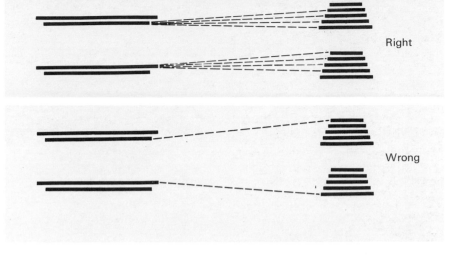

Right

Wrong

with a 13-14-15-17-19-21 freewheel.

The most expensive, and still the best, gear system is the Campagnolo Super Record with titanium components. It is somewhat lighter than the Campagnolo Nuovo Record, which is quite a lot cheaper and almost as good. Other good gears come from Shimano, Simplex, Huret, Sun Tour and Zeus. There is not a lot to choose between them in weight (see table). Don't be persuaded into buying cheap gearing, because in the long run it can develop problems. With the front changer, the same companies manufacture matching models, all of which can happily handle a 12-tooth difference between chainrings. Both front and rear changing

mechanisms need to be precisely adjusted so that the chain can't travel too far inwards or outwards and fall off the chainrings on the inside or outside, dropping between the smallest sprocket and the frame, or between the largest sprocket and the spokes. The gear control levers are usually fastened to the down tube, but there are also handlebar controls, which plug into the handlebar ends instead

Gear levers.

Campagnolo.

Sun Tour.

Simplex.

Weight of various gear mechanisms

Mechanism	Weight
Campagnolo Super Record (titanium)	180g
Campagnolo Nuovo Record (duralumin)	205g
Shimano 600	190g
Shimano Dura-Ace 600	190g
Sun Tour Cyclone	200g
Simplex Super LJ	225g

43

of the normal plugs. This type of control is popular with cyclo-cross riders, but road sprint specialists sometimes choose them, because they can change gear during finishing sprints without taking their hands from the bars.

Campagnolo Super Record.

Campagnolo Nuovo Record.

Shimano 600.

Campagnolo Super Record.

Shimano 600 EX.

Accessories

Never try to save money on your pump and spare tyre, for these are vital accessories. Drinking bottle and cage are useful, and there is much to be said for fitting an odometer.

Pump
The pump is usually fitted between the top tube and the bottom bracket housing, running down the inside of the seat tube. Provided that the pump is the right length, there is no need for any special attaching apparatus. Racing pumps are usually of plastic, because this weighs less than steel. And for workshop use, or taking in the boot of the car to a race, a track pump with a pressure gauge is worth having.

Spare tubular tyre.

Pump.

Spare tyre

As previously recommended, you should carry at least one spare tyre, strapped underneath the saddle. The spare tyre should have been previously used, and should be tightly rolled up and wrapped before being put under the saddle. The wrapping is important, because a soaked tyre won't easily stick to the rim.

Bottle cage

The bottle cage is fitted on the down tube, either with clips or bolted to brazed-on bosses on the frame itself. These are of alloy or titanium, weighing around 50g. For time trials, hill climbs or criteriums, bottle cages aren't needed, and so can be removed.

Drinking bottle

Racing cyclists use drinking bottles made of plastic. In the cap they have a tiny plug, which you can pull out with your teeth during a race. Normal capacity is a half-litre. For cold weather, there are special insulated bottles rather like Thermos flasks, but they contain less. Because of the fashion for lowering wind resistance, you can even get aerodynamic bottles!

Drinking bottle and cage.

Odometer

For cycle racing an odometer is superfluous, but it can be really useful during training, when it can tell you how far you have ridden, even giving extra motivation as a result. A simple odometer is usually fixed to the front hub axle. There are two basic models, one with a striker fixed to one spoke, gradually turning a cog-wheel on the odometer itself and making a clicking noise. The other drives the odometer reading by a thin rubber belt.

Assembling a racing cycle

1. The frame is selected (picture 1), then the bottom bracket shell, head tube and seat tube reamed out (pictures 2 and 3).
2. The bottom bracket is lubricated with special grease, then fitted (pictures 4 and 5).
3. The cranks and chainrings are fitted (picture 6).
4. The head set is fitted (pictures 7–9).
5. The gear levers are fixed to the down tube and the cables inserted (picture 10).
6. The rear mechanism is bolted on (picture 11), then the front changer (picture 12). The cables are attached (picture 13).
7. The brake stirrups are bolted to the frame (picture 14).
8. The wheels are spoked and trued (pictures 15 and 16).
9. Several coats of rim cement are built up (picture 17) and the tubulars stretched on to the rim (picture 18).
10. The freewheel and quick-release are fitted to the wheels (picture 21).
11. The wheels are fitted to the frame (picture 20).
12. The chain length is measured (picture 19) and riveted (picture 22).
13. The stem is fitted to the bars (picture 23) and the handlebar

assembly fitted into the frame (picture 24).

14. The brake levers are fitted to the bars (picture 25).
15. The brake cables are fitted (picture 26) and the brakes adjusted (picture 27).
16. The seat pin (picture 28) and saddle (picture 29) are fitted.
17. The pedals, toe-clips and straps are fitted (picture 30).
18. The bottle cage is mounted (picture 31).
19. The handlebars are taped (picture 32).
20. The finished machine (picture 33).

The chain should be kept in tension either with a piece of wood or by a special fixing apparatus.

The fixing bolts of the brakes.

The moving parts of the front changer.

Maintenance of the machine

The racing cycle is a very expensive piece of precision engineering. It is of course vulnerable to sheer brute force, but it is built to withstand much of the assaults of the weather. Neither aluminium nor titanium-alloy frames or components are susceptible to rust.

All the same, it needs regular maintenance. Many top riders will come in from a long rainy outing and see to their machines before they start to look after themselves. Discipline and dedication to cycle sport are displayed not only in concern for the body, but also in the way a racing cycle is cared for. It is nevertheless a simple enough task, for which you need a little petrol, a small and a large brush, a bucket of soapy water, and a sponge.

You first put some washing-up liquid into a bucket of warm water, then remove both wheels from the frame. Make sure that the chain doesn't scratch the chain stay by keeping it in tension, either by using a special brazed-on fitment on which it can hang, or by putting a long piece of wood through the triangular opening of the rear drop-outs. Wash the spokes, hubs and rims with a sponge, the tyres with a soft brush, then dry them off with an absorbent cloth. This is important, for the cotton thread of which most tyre carcasses are made does not like the damp. It can rot and become very weak. After this, put the wheels on one side.

The rear gear parts . . .

the freewheel . . .

and the chain should be lubricated with petrol.

Then give the brakes and gear mechanisms a light once-over with the small brush which has been dipped in petrol, to stop water getting in so easily. Then wash the frame with the sponge and soapy water. If you use a detergent containing silicone you can shine the frame and accessories at the same time, without having to dry them off. Headsets, bracket sets and hubs are usually pretty well sealed, so you don't have to worry about getting water out and regreasing them.

If the chain is really dirty, give it a special clean with the petrol brush before you start to clean the bicycle proper. Then very lightly grease it.

After washing the bike, lubricate the freewheel, laying the rear wheel down horizontally and then spinning the freewheel with your fingers to let the oil circulate.

Then put a few drops of oil on the cables, on the arms of the gears and the moving parts of the brake stirrups.

The hubs need to be stripped down only once a year, and packed with special hub grease, such as Campagnolo.

Maintaining your machine gets the best out of the material and helps to identify problems at an early stage. You might find that the brake stirrups are pulling unevenly, the gears need adjusting, the chain is getting slack through wear, or there is a crack in the toe-clip which could lead to eventual breakage. Apart from this, there is a psychological boost in going out training on a bike in tip-top condition, sparkling clean, and mechanically reliable.

Useful maintenance and small repairs

The most important tools:

1. Screwdriver
2. Wire cutters
3. 5mm allen key
4. 6mm allen key and 8mm socket spanner
5. 10/11mm spanner
6. Crank extractor
7. Ring-spanner for axle bolts
8. Chain riveter
9. Spoke key
10. Cone spanner
11. Spanner for bottom bracket adjusting cup and for headset
12. Spanner for fixed cup and for pedal
13. Spanner for bottom bracket lockring and headset

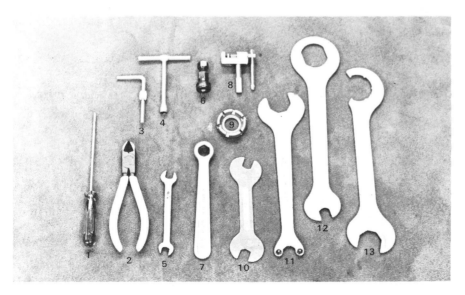

1

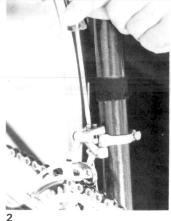

2

3

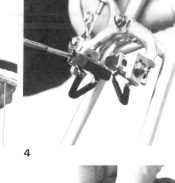

4

5

6

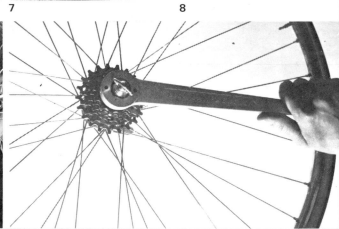

7

8

9

10

11

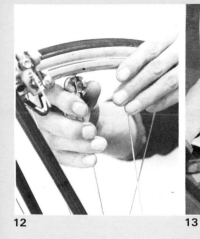

12

13

14

15

16

17

18

19

Most important maintenance tasks

1. Adjusting the rear gear mechanism (picture 1).
2. Adjusting the front changer (picture 2).
3. Adjusting the brakes (picture 3).
4. Changing the brake blocks: push out the old blocks with a screwdriver (picture 4) and then slide in the new brake blocks (picture 5).
5. Putting new cement on the rim (picture 6) and fitting the tyre (picture 7).
6. Changing the chain (perhaps every 2000km). Picture 8 shows a worn and stretched chain. Pictures 9 and 10 show the fitting and riveting of a new chain.
7. Removing the freewheel (picture 11).
8. Truing the wheels. Rough truing while the wheel is in the frame (picture 12) or in a wheel-truing stand (picture 13).
9. Regular lubrication at various points (pictures 14–19).

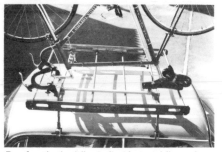

Roof rack; the bike is fixed at saddle and handlebars

Roof rack with fixings at front forks and rear wheel, the normal way of transporting bikes.

Transporting your bike

Once it was normal to cycle long distances to races. Nowadays that has changed, and there are some very good reasons why the bike goes by car with its rider. If you live in the centre of a city, it makes sense to drive out to quieter roads before you take to the bike. You might use the car to get you to a different training area, or want to take your bike on holiday. Some people love to go climbing hillside roads, and it would be impractical to ride a bicycle to the foot of the hills first. The simplest way of taking your bike with you is to take the wheels off and put them and the rest of the machine into the boot. Doing just this amount of disassembly (and it is quickly reassembled) means that a bike can be taken in virtually every small car. You could even put the frame on the back seat and the wheels behind it, or in the boot. It

is always advisable, however, to protect the tyres with special tyre covers, and not put heavy items on top of the frame or the wheels. But when, because of luggage or other passengers, there is no room for the bike inside the car or in the boot, you have to think of a carrying rack with special cycle attachments. On a roof rack you can carry several bikes at once. There are two basic types: one which takes the bicycle upside down, securing it at the handlebars and the saddle; in the other, the machine is held upright, the rear wheel in a channel and secured by a toe-strap, the front wheel removed and placed in a special fork-like fitment, and the front forks secured by a quick-release fitment to the rack. When it comes to really expensive machines, only the second type of rack can be considered, because one can never secure the upside-down type as firmly; the bike is bound

to sway about while the car is in motion. The other disadvantage is that saddle and handlebars can sometimes be marked by their contact with the fitment. With both types of rack, several bikes can be carried, depending on the rack's design and the size of the car.

Important:
Because of the wind resistance offered by bikes on roof racks, it's best to keep speed below 120kph.

The most important pieces of cycle-racing clothing.

Clothing

The clothing of riders in recognized races is covered by regulations, both of national federations and of the Union Cycliste Internationale (UCI), the world governing body.
Road-racing riders must wear the following:

- ☐ Cycling shoes
- ☐ White ankle socks
- ☐ Short black racing shorts
- ☐ Racing jersey
- ☐ Crash-hat or helmet

In track races the socks are not necessary, and regulations in Britain allow time trials to be ridden without protective headgear.
To these compulsory items can be added the following recommendations:

- ☐ Racing cap
- ☐ Track mitts
- ☐ Undervest

In rainy weather it's often advisable to take a racing cape (waterproof lightweight jacket) in the back pocket of your jersey. For special events such as time trials you can wear a one-piece 'skinsuit' which hugs the contours of the body.

The racing jersey

A typical road-racing jersey is made either of pure wool or of a mixture of wool and acrylic fibre, the latter easier to care for. A jersey should be slightly stretchy, allowing the body to breathe, and soak up its sweat. It should fit the body closely without constricting it, and should not flap about in the wind. When the rider is bent over the handlebars, the jersey should be long enough to cover the lower back, to guard against the kidney area getting chilled. There are jerseys with short or long sleeves, to be worn according to the weather. There are even arm warmers, which you can put on with a short-sleeve jersey during a race or a training run.

Jerseys usually have three and sometimes five pockets, the three being at the back, where you can conveniently put race food. There are sometimes chest pockets too, but these tend to become bulky and are an irritant when riding. For special events such as track, time trials, circuit races or hill climbs, you can wear silk jerseys, because of the lowered wind resistance of this fibre.
Racing jerseys are best washed in cold water and a mild washing powder. One final point. There are rules governing the size of lettering on shorts and jerseys, and these need to be considered.

Sidi Titanium shoes with narrow last. They have replaceable shoe-plates.

Duegi shoes with wooden inserts, wooden soles and replaceable shoe-plates.

Adidas Merckx Super shoes. The upper is of nylon mesh, which gives good ventilation. The plates are tacked to the soles.

Racing shoes

The racing shoe is probably the most important piece of clothing for the competitive cyclist. Just work out what it means to cover perhaps 20,000km in a year, riding gears of average 80in (see page 86) — something like three million pedal revolutions! The racing shoe transmits the leg thrust to the pedal, the greatest load being around the area of the big toe joint.

A good cycling shoe should fulfil the following criteria:

☐ It must fit the foot closely without impeding the circulation.
☐ It should have a stiff perforated sole.
☐ It must be light.
☐ It must blend into a unit (via shoe plates fixed to its sole) with the pedal, toe-clips and straps.

Because of the importance of racing shoes, the cyclist should never seek to save money here. The uppers should be soft, of box-calf leather, and should have holes to allow the foot to breathe. To the uppers should be sewn a soft, supple tongue. Specially firm laces should be used, taken through seven or eight lace-holes. The sole should be as stiff as possible, most shoes having a leather sole with steel insert. More recently, some shoes have used an artificial resin sole strengthened with glass-fibre insert.

Because of the important role the shoe plays in transmitting leg-power, it is vital not to walk in racing shoes if it can be avoided. This only serves to soften and bend the sole. This is why racing men usually don their shoes just before a race, and take them off straight afterwards.

It is very important to fit the shoe-plates correctly, or at least to place adjustable shoe-plates correctly. From this placing comes good riding style and economical pedalling action. Because racing shoes must be a close fit, it is worth buying them a half-size too small and letting them gradually stretch to fit properly, with sweat and damp. One way of doing this is to ease on the new shoe, then stand in lukewarm water, and immediately go out on a training ride. This is how to tailor your own shoes to a perfect fit! It goes without saying that you must look after your shoes. If they've had a soaking, stuff them with newspaper and let them dry out naturally. Never put a wet shoe next to direct heat, or the leather will become cracked and brittle. No, better to let the shoe dry naturally, then give it a good brushing and finally use a high-quality shoe cream or polish.

Shoe-plates are of steel, aluminium or plastic. Without them the shoe will slide around on the pedal, even with the straps pulled tight. Your foot can come out of the pedal involuntarily, and many unfortunate souls have scraped their shins on the toothed edge of the pedal as a result. Shoes with built-in adjustable shoe-plates are heavier, but you can get the position right much more easily.

Socks

Socks should be white, short, and close-fitting. Normally they come not far above the ankles. They are best in wool or cotton. Coloured socks not only look wrong on a racing cyclist, they are also against the rules.

Shorts

Racing shorts with a chamois leather insert are another important article of clothing. They are made of wool or synthetic fibre, with the insert of finest chamois. They are worn next to the skin. The length of the leg should be sufficient to stop the inside of the thigh rubbing against the saddle. Once again, they should be close-fitting, but not tight enough to affect the circulation. The waist elastic should not be too narrow, and in fact shorts are best worn not with elastic but with light braces, worn over the undervest but underneath the racing jersey. Woollen shorts above all should be washed in cool water, so that the material does not felt. For the same reason they should be allowed to dry naturally — not on the radiator! After drying the chamois should be lubricated with Vaseline or a special chamois fat made for this purpose. This way it will recover its suppleness. Without this regular care you can get a lot of saddle soreness.

Shorts have appeared recently in very thin clinging material

Cycle-racing shorts with chamois insert.

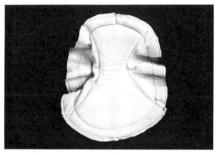

Insert of the finest material.

Bib shorts in light, 'breathing' material.

which is easy to wear. There are also shorts which have their own built-in braces of the same material ('bib shorts'). The advantage is in the close fit, the resultant aerodynamic qualities, and the fact of being easy to care for. But they do cost more than ordinary shorts.

Protective headgear

The crash-hat is for head protection in the event of an upset. It is made out of padded leather bars and held fast by a strap under the chin. You must wear a crash-hat of some kind in all road and track races. There are also all-over helmets made from plastic, which are lighter, ventilated, and better protection

Leather crash-hat.

Plastic crash-helmet.

for the head. But in hot conditions they are not as easy to wear.

Racing cap

A racing cap is made from cotton, and is designed to give some

Cotton racing cap.

protection against the sun's rays. The famous Italian rider Gino Bartali 'improved' the cap's design in great heat by putting a large cabbage leaf underneath, which hung down over his neck at the back!
The other purpose is to soak up sweat, which would otherwise run down the forehead into the eyes.

Gloves

Racing gloves, otherwise known as 'track mitts' because track riders use them for a brake on the tyre tread, are made from soft leather and fabric. The fingers are short, the back generally of crochet or net material, the palm of padded soft leather, often chamois. This moderate padding

Track mitts with leather palm and crochet back.

cushions the shocks from the handlebars, and stops the palms blistering on long rides. They are also invaluable in crashes, when they protect the delicate palm area. There are also mitts made entirely of leather, generally thicker, because they are used as substitute brakes by trackmen, who of course ride machines without brakes. Even the

Leather track mitts give a better grip on the bars, and protect the hands in the event of a crash.

roadman puts his gloved hand on the tyre tread sometimes, to clean off small stones or other foreign bodies which might cause punctures.

Undervest

Under racing shorts nothing should be worn, but an undervest is necessary under a racing jersey. It might be a cotton vest with short sleeves, or perhaps another racing jersey without pockets. In cool weather it's a good idea to slip several layers of newspaper, or a plastic bag, down the front of the jersey, to keep the cold wind off the chest. There are even special chest protectors made from a windproof material, open at the sides and the back, which serve the same protective purpose.

Racing cape

In cold and rainy weather racing cyclists take with them a rain jacket made of wind and waterproof plastic. The front has a Velcro fastening, and the garment is longer at the back to protect the lower back down to

Waterproof and windproof plastic racing cape keeps the damp out and the warmth in. The side panels are for ventilation.

saddle level. Rolled up, this racing cape goes into a jersey pocket. It serves the double purpose of protection from the wet and the cold, and for this reason riders seldom use one in warm rainy weather, because otherwise they would sweat too much.

Aerodynamic suit

This is a one-piece suit which has a long front zip from navel to neck. The material is a silky synthetic type which clings to the body. Such a 'skinsuit' is light to wear and offers less wind resistance than normal racing clothing.
It is mostly used for time trials, hill climbs and cyclo-cross,

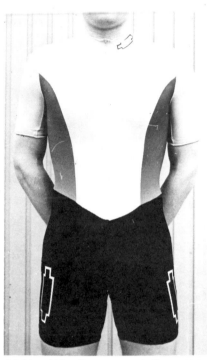

A 'skinsuit' in silky man-made fibre which hugs the body and lowers wind resistance.

basically events where the rider does not need jersey pockets. The material is close-woven, but it lets the skin breathe and allows sweat to evaporate.
Cycle-racing clothing has been developed for a special purpose, and has proved its worth over the years. A leisure rider can only benefit from wearing some or all of these items. Racing shorts with a chamois insert, and good racing

shoes, are certainly ideal for any long ride, and track mitts, racing cap and jersey can be very useful too.

Training clothing

In summer
In the summer you should train in race clothing. The bright colours of

Cycle sport clothing for summer: racing cap in cotton, short-sleeved wool or wool/acrylic mixture racing jersey, undervest of cotton or wool. Track mitts. Racing shorts with chamois insert, white socks, racing shoes with shoe-plates.

a racing jersey can be seen from a long way off, and this is a safety aid. If you go on long rides which involve a lot of climbing or hill roads, then it is good to take a spare undervest with you. You can

Spring and autumn clothing: long-sleeved woollen or wool/acrylic mixture jersey, cotton or wool undervest, with a folded newspaper or chest protector in between. In colder weather a woollen jersey on top. Long training tights with racing shorts underneath, held up by braces. As a guard against suddenly worsening weather, a racing cape in the jersey pocket. In the immediate post-season period, arm warmers and leg warmers may suffice.

come to the top of a long climb sweating profusely, and then get chilled descending if you don't stop at the top to put on a dry vest. The alternative is to put some folded newspaper up the front of your jersey.

In spring, autumn and winter
In these seasons, especially when the temperature falls below 5°C, there are two vulnerable points, the hands and the feet. You protect the hands with thick knitted gloves which are warm but let the air through. You can protect your feet by adding overshoes, in plastic, vinyl or rubber, which will also protect against the wet. Many professionals use normal racing shoes during the winter, but pull thick woollen socks over the top of them. There are also special winter shoes for racing, which are lined with real or simulated sheepskin.
On the upper body you wear several layers of racing jerseys, and in extreme cold you can start with a woollen vest, add one or two woollen jerseys, and top them off with a windproof racing cape. Your legs can be covered with long woollen training bottoms, under which you wear normal racing shorts. The alternative is knee-length training trousers (plus-

Winter clothing: woollen cap which can be pulled down over the ears. Long-sleeved wool or wool/acrylic jersey; underneath a wool or cotton undervest and a cotton sweater. When necessary, a racing cape on top. Warm gloves, long woollen training tights over racing shorts. According to the weather, either shoe-covers over normal racing shoes (or pull a pair of socks over them) or special winter shoes with fur lining.

twos) with long woollen stockings. Ordinary tracksuits aren't very good in very cold weather because they let too much wind through. Your head should be covered with a woolly hat which can be pulled down to cover the ears. Normal racing caps are too flimsy, offering no protection against the wind and soon getting soaked with sweat. This in turn is made icy cold by the wind, and once again you risk a chill. If you're dressed properly you can train even in freezing conditions.

The man on the bicycle

In training and races, a competitive cyclist spends many hours in the saddle. For this reason you can only get the best from yourself if the position on the bike is just right, giving you the optimum riding style. One of the best stylists of recent years has been Germany's Dietrich Thurau, who held the yellow jersey in the 1978 Tour de France and in doing so was designated the event's most elegant rider. Good riding style gives a feeling of balance and above all of ease. It allows the complete, almost effortless use of available power. Since two men are never identical in their stride, it's impossible to have two riders identical in riding style and position. Each rider has his own peculiarities, depending on his build. But there are basic principles which apply to every rider. Optimal riding style depends on correct saddle position and how well you pedal. I'll now go on to deal with finding saddle position. The principle of good pedalling is dealt with in the section on *The secret of round pedalling* (page 67).

The right saddle position

If you have your saddle position right, then without stretching or cramping yourself you will be able to make all the necessary movements of the upper body, whether it is on the flat, climbing hills, or in a sprint finish. You should not have to waste energy correcting your position needlessly during a race by using your arms to shift yourself back and forward on the saddle. Ideally the body weight should be distributed so that 55 per cent rests on the rear wheel and 45 per cent on the front.
The pedal stroke should be powerful and yet easy. When the pedal reaches its lowest point the knee should not be fully extended, otherwise the smooth movement of the limb is hindered. There will be aches in the muscles, premature exhaustion, and saddle soreness. Good pedalling is impossible this way. If, however, your saddle is too low, then the thigh will be able to bend too much on the upstroke; it will keep hitting your diaphragm and your breathing will be hindered.
Good riding position starts with the selection of the frame,

making sure that the size and top tube length are right, that the crank length suits your leg length and the general build of the body. We must assume that these are right first, before starting to find the ideal position, balancing the following four variable factors:

☐ Saddle height
☐ Saddle position
☐ Reach
☐ Height of handlebars

Saddle height
First set your saddle height approximately. You can work out what it should be, taking the measurement from the centre of the bottom bracket axle to the theoretical point where the extended seat tube meets the surface of the saddle. You take $6/7$ of the leg length (measured from hip bone to sole) and deduct 1 cm. For a leg length of 91 cm the distance from saddle surface to bottom bracket axle would be: $(91 \times 6/7) - 1 = 78 - 1 = 77$ cm. Now you sit on the saddle and make the following tests, in order to get the position exactly right:

Fixing the saddle height. **1**   **2**   **3**

1. Put your feet in the toe-clips, with the cranks in the vertical position. The 'straight' leg should not in fact be stretched, but should, instead, be in a slightly bent attitude, say 175°.

2. Put your toes underneath the lower pedal. If the foot is now parallel to the ground and the leg is fully extended, then the saddle height is right.

3. Flick the lower pedal over, so that the toe-clip is underneath, and put your heel on the pedal. Once again, the leg should now be quite extended.

Once the saddle height has been set, you should find the seat pillar is 8 to 11cm out of the frame. If it is more or less, then your frame size isn't ideal.

Saddle inclination
Normally the saddle should be exactly horizontal, parallel with the top tube. But if you have the feeling that, while riding, you have the tendency to slide forward and have to keep pushing yourself back with your arms, then you can tilt the saddle nose upwards very slightly.

61

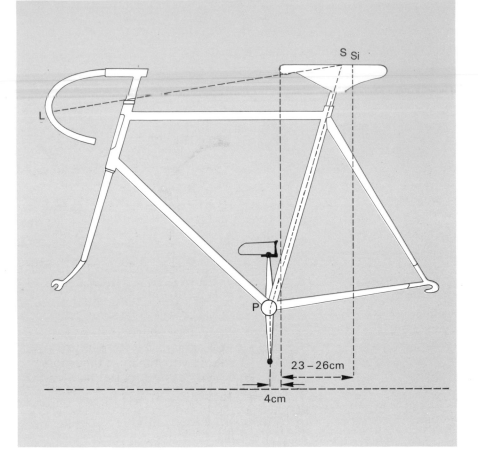

Ways of setting the saddle and handlebar positions. A line dropped from the front of the saddle should fall 2–5cm (average 4cm) behind the centre of the bottom bracket. A line from the point on the saddle where the ischial bones rest should lie 23–26cm behind the centre of the bottom bracket. The reach (S–L) generally matches the saddle height (S–P).

Saddle position

It only remains to correct the saddle position by forward or backward adjustment. With a road bike, the saddle nose is generally between 2 and 5cm (average 4cm) behind a line falling through the bottom bracket axle. Similarly, if a line is dropped from the point on the saddle where the pelvic bones make contact, it will be 23 to 26cm behind that point. So set your saddle this way to start with, set the cranks horizontal, put your feet in the clips, and adopt the racing position. In this position, a line from the front of the forward kneecap should fall through the pedal axle. Some riders prefer to adopt a position slightly more forward, however, so that the line falls between axle and the front pedal plate.

Reach

This is the measurement from the back of the saddle to the nearest part of the handlebar. Generally speaking, the distance from the saddle surface where the extended seat tube would meet it to the farthest part of the handlebar bend is the same as the saddle height. For exact positioning of the reach you adopt the racing position, your hands gripping the dropped part of the bars, and your arms slightly bent. Now set the cranks parallel to the down tube. In this position the upper knee should just overlap the bent elbow (see picture). If you need a stem longer than 12 to 15cm, then the frame is too short.

Handlebar height

The handlebar tops should never be higher than the saddle. Start off with them at the same height, and as your training proceeds gradually lower the bars, but they should never be more than 4cm lower than the saddle.
One exception to this would be if you have very long arms. In this

Checking the reach. In the racing position, holding the dropped part of the bars, the knee should just overlap the elbow when the crank is parallel to the down tube.

case you can lower the bars a little more.

Important: If your bars are too low, then you will no longer be able to breathe properly.
Once you have found your own ideal position via these measurements and tests, try it out on a gentle training ride, to see whether the position 'works' in actual riding conditions. Once you have established that it is

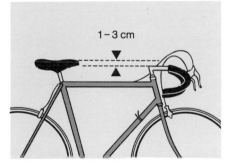

Handlebar height: the bar should never be higher than the saddle, and according to your state of fitness will be 1–3cm lower than the saddle.

right, then you should put down the resultant measurements on a diagram (see our example) so that if you buy a new bicycle to replace your old or stolen machine you will have all the relevant data to hand.

Good riding style

If your riding style is right, then you'll feel good on the bike. Once a rider has a feeling for this style, his performance will improve and so will his enjoyment and desire to ride more. There can be no success without good riding style.
The principle is that a rider, with the help of his own muscle strength, must overcome three types of resisting forces: air resistance, rolling resistance, and gravity. The competitor must try to minimize these three forces, and to master them with the most economical power output on his behalf. Essentially, **air resistance** becomes greater with increasing speed, the resistance growing by the square of that increase. This factor is affected by the surface presented to the wind. Good riding style makes this frontal area as small as possible, ensuring again that breathing is not impaired, or the physical input reduced. It is more important to find the most streamlined position when you are travelling at higher speeds, say in a time trial or a breakaway attempt.

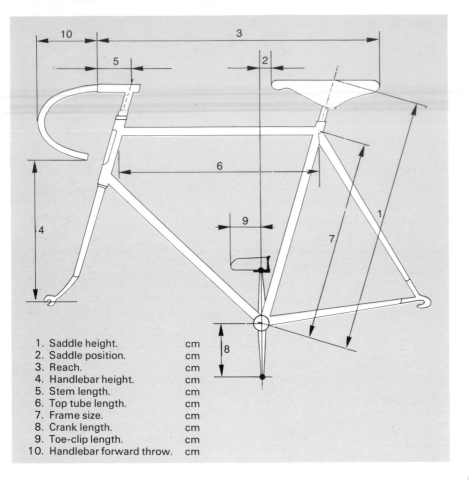

1. Saddle height.   cm
2. Saddle position.   cm
3. Reach.   cm
4. Handlebar height.   cm
5. Stem length.   cm
6. Top tube length.   cm
7. Frame size.   cm
8. Crank length.   cm
9. Toe-clip length.   cm
10. Handlebar forward throw.   cm

the head. In the lowest position the head 'disappears' in front of the body, which itself is considerably reduced (see illustration). If you reckon up the various frontal areas, then you find that the highest position gives a reading of $0.6m^2$, the medium $0.5m^2$, and the lowest position $0.3m^2$. This means that riding in the high position at 30 kilometres per hour you experience the same wind resistance as in the low position at 45 kilometres per hour. As your speed increases, you should streamline your position more and more. For each position on the bike, there are different ways of holding the handlebars. With

You can assess a rider's frontal area with the aid of photos, converting the images to more basic geometric shapes for consideration. Basically a rider adopts three different positions. The highest one, sitting with hands on top of the handlebars; the medium, typical racing position; and the lowest, very streamlined. The frontal area is composed of the bicycle as seen from the front, the torso, legs and

When you have found the ideal position on your machine, the correct measurements should be noted on a chart such as this.

Frontal area using different positions.   ▷
1. High position, hands holding the tops of the bars.
2. Middle position, hands holding the brake lever hoods.
3. Low position, hands holding the drops.

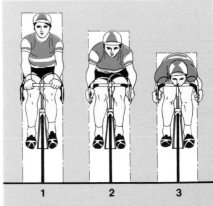

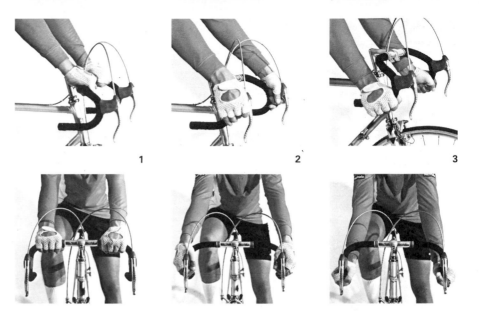

1 2 3

the highest position, you ride 'on the tops'. In the medium position you frequently ride with hands holding the brake lever hoods, and in the lowest position your hands are holding the dropped part of the bars (see illustration). Part of an aerodynamic position is an economic leg action. The legs move in two parallel planes as close as possible to the frame, the knees sometimes even brushing the top tube. This ideal leg action is only possible if the feet are correctly placed on the pedals. This is when the big toe joint — the ball of the foot — is directly over the pedal axle. Through the use of shoe-plates, clips and straps, the foot becomes a single unit with the pedal. This presupposes that the toe-clips are the right length, which means that the front of the shoe will not quite touch the clip, but that there will be a gap of 2 to 3mm. The point at which the shoe-plates are attached to the shoe sole is dictated to a certain extent by the toe-clip length. This point can be found empirically, by going out on a long ride in newly-bought shoes, and then studying the imprint made on the sole by the plates of the pedal cage. Where the rear plate has

made its mark should be the position of the shoe-plate slot. It is important that the foot should lie at right angles to the pedal axle, otherwise the toes might point in — or worst of all, out. The foot should be able to work in parallel with the plane of the frame, an essential part of good riding style.

Good riding style consists of the correct seat position, an aerodynamic position with the correct placing of the hands on the bars, and of the feet on the pedals. The arms should be slightly bent, to absorb some of the shock and jolting from the road surface.

Holding the bars:
1. On the tops: relaxed grip, easy breathing, for gentle riding and easy climbs.
2. On the hoods: comfortable grip, but frontal area somewhat reduced, used when making some effort but in someone's slipstream, and always ready to brake. For use on steeper climbs and in rolling country.
3. On the drops: deepest position with lowest wind resistance, only comfortable for fit riders, used when riding at speed, into a wind, in breakaway attempts or sprinting.

Good position on the bike. The back is arched, the hands are on the drops, the arms are slightly bent at the elbow, the legs moving up and down close to the frame.

You must always have the feeling of being relaxed on the bike. Once all these points have been satisfied, there are three other essentials, which have to be mastered and kept under constant control:

1. You must make sure that your legs work in exact parallel, like two piston rods.
2. A perfect stylist lets the legs do the work, the rest of the body not moving. Above all, the head should be kept still and the body should not bob up and down or from side to side. This point has exceptions during sprinting and hill-climbing.
3. The leg strength should be smoothly passed on to the transmission. The resulting movement of the legs is called 'round pedalling'.

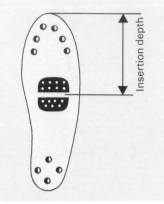

Insertion depth of the racing shoe.

Placing of the foot on the pedal. The long axis of the foot should be at 90° to the pedal axle, or occasionally slightly pointed inwards — but never outwards!

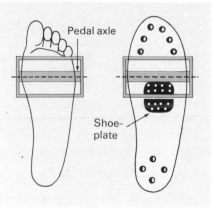

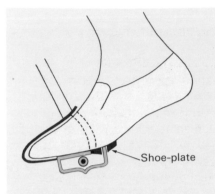

Foot in the toe-clip: there should be a gap of 2–3mm between the toe-clip and the toe of the shoe.

Foot in the toe-clip. Be careful where the toe-strap buckle is placed.

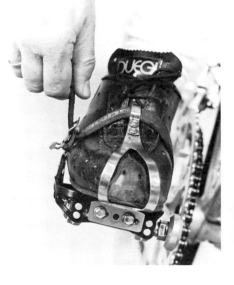

The secret of round pedalling

Good pedalling action distinguishes the experienced racing cyclist. Only through countless turns of the pedals is such an action learned, and it may be a comfort to know that even top professionals have to rediscover their pedalling action, their *coup de pedale,* at the start of every season.

What's so difficult about it? Why can't you just get on the bike and push down on the pedals? The laws of physics dictate that force acting on a lever (in this case the cranks) is most efficient when it acts at right angles to that lever. When it comes to pedalling, this means that force is most efficiently used if it is always applied at right angles to the crank, whatever position it may be in. When the pedal is on the downstroke the effective angle of energy input alters constantly, until when the cranks are vertical it is 0°, this point being called 'top dead centre'. Seen simply, this kind of movement can never produce a completely perfect transmission of energy into motion.

In ideal pedalling action, pulling

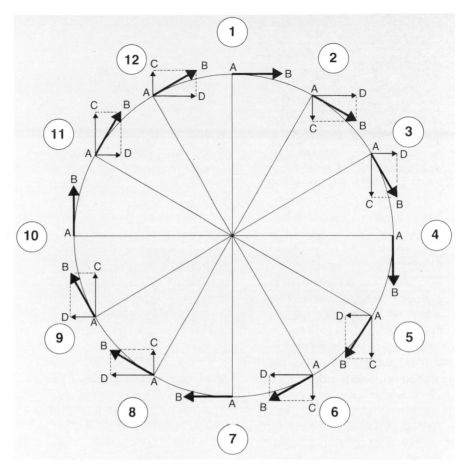

and pushing forces are used, always at right angles to the crank. The perfect pedaller is always seeking to approach this ideal. He reaches it if he can proportion the up-and-down forces of his legs with those pushing the pedals forward and backwards, so that at any point in the revolution there is an equal amount of force being applied, and as close to that right angle as possible. You can split the pedal revolution into several sections.

The optimal division of pedalling forces. In each phase of the pedal revolution the horizontal (A–D) and vertical (A C) forces should be in a certain proportion, so that the resulting force (A–B) should be working at right angles to the cranks, and thus have the best possible effect. The length of the lines indicates the size of the forces illustrated. The force of leverage should ideally always be perpendicular to the crank.

Let's divide it into four, a convenient way to illustrate the points I have made.

1. The critical top sector, at 'top dead centre'. Force acting mainly in a forward direction.
2. The sector with the best energy input, the direction of the force mainly downwards.
3. The critical low sector 'bottom dead centre', the toes coming into play and the direction of the force mainly rearwards.
4. The sector with the worst energy input, the force directed into pulling upwards.

Because good pedalling style is so critical, though, we can even split the pedal revolution into 12 sectors, like a clock-face (see illustration on previous page). In each position of the pedals the corresponding parallelogram of forces is set out. The lines A–C represent the vertical forces (downwards or upwards); lines A–D symbolize the horizontal forces (working forwards from behind or backwards from the front). Arrow A–B shows the ideal direction of force.

If the pedal is at top dead centre (point 1) there is no vertical force acting downwards. At this point the pedal must be pressed forward. To do this, the front of the foot is slightly raised, and the pushing movement comes from the thigh extensors and the flexors of the foot.

At point 2 the forward pressure is lessened, and a small amount of downward vertical effort (A–C) is exerted.

At point 3 the forward pressure is reduced still further as the vertical pressure is increased. The foot is now almost horizontal.

At point 4 there is only downward pressure.

There is still this downward pressure at point 5, but some horizontal force, working towards the rear, is introduced, thanks to the flexors at the back of the thigh and of the gluteals.

The pull backwards is greater at point 6, more so than the downward pressure. This is achieved by dropping the toe.

At point 7, bottom dead centre, only the horizontal force, working backwards, is in play. In this position the ankle is fully extended, the toes pointing as far downwards as possible, and the thigh starts to flex.

At point 8 the backwards pressure is continued, but a vertical upwards force now begins to work. The toe is still pointing downwards, but the thigh is now lifting, with the help of the hip flexors.

At point 9 the upward vertical force is increasing, while the rearward pull is diminishing.

At point 10 only the upward vertical force is acting.

At point 11 the pedal is still being pulled upwards, but a forward pressure is now coming into action.

At point 12 the upward pull is reduced, but the forward pressure is distinctly increased.

You can see from these periodical parallelograms of force that the energy put into the pedals is constant, and each time acts at right angles to the crank. Of course you can't concentrate on this idea while you are pedalling, but it is good, at least once, to see a single turn of the pedal broken up like this. Only when you understand the theory can you practise it properly.

The most important part of the body for a good pedalling action is the foot. It performs an easy up-and-down movement, with the ankle joint as the axis. During the pedal revolution the toes point up and down. This demands great mobility of the ankle, especially when the rider is using a high gear, or is climbing a hill. The faster the pedalling rate, the smaller the lift of the toes around

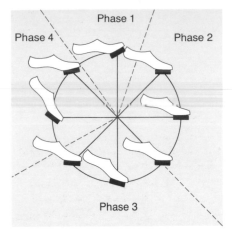

Phase 1
Phase 4
Phase 2
Phase 3

Low pedalling rate (60–90rpm). On climbs, mountains, time trials etc. Typical is the lifting of the toe at top dead centre and the dropping of the toe at bottom dead centre.

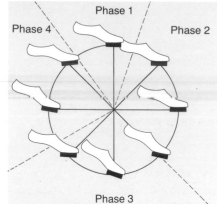

Phase 1
Phase 4
Phase 2
Phase 3

Medium pedalling rate (90–110rpm). For racing in the bunch etc. The foot remains virtually horizontal during the upper sector, or the toe drops slightly.

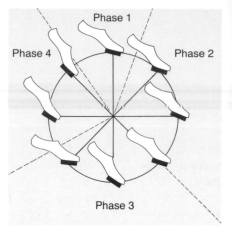

Phase 1
Phase 4
Phase 2
Phase 3

High pedalling rate (110–150rpm). Sprints, track events. The speed of the foot itself takes it past top dead centre. At all points the toe is more or less pointed downwards.

top dead centre. At this point the foot becomes increasingly horizontal, and at high pedalling rates can even point downwards. You learn good pedalling by consciously following through the ankle movement and watching how the foot behaves. At first you do this at a very low pedalling rate, then you gradually increase the cadence and at the same time try to keep the ankle movement going. You must of course try to keep the ankle joint relaxed. To get the best idea of how good your pedalling style is, try pedalling with one foot only. Take the left foot out of the clip and pedal just with the right, or vice versa, trying to keep constant power going. In this way you can feel in which direction you need to push or pull. After a few hundred metres change feet.

Once you have mastered the right style pedalling with one foot, you should practise with both feet. It is particularly important to lift the leg in the second part of the revolution, remembering that a leg is equal to about one-fifth of body weight. Similarly, as you are pushing forward and down with one foot, you must think of pulling backwards and upwards with the other.

The quality of a cyclist lies less in the sheer power he can pour into the pedals, and more in having a good, round pedalling style at a fast rate. At least, that is true when riding on the flat. The strength comes into it in sprints, breakaway efforts, or long climbs. For leisure riders a decent pedalling rate is 50-60rpm. This isn't the case for racing cyclists. Usually it is much higher,

between 90 and 110. In track events you can reach pedalling rates of 120 to 150rpm. The greatest test of a bike-rider's ability is the world hour record, which has been set in several attempts at a pedalling rate of 103-108rpm. No one would expect that any such record ride could have been successful with faulty technique, so we can therefore accept that this unanimously chosen rate of just over 100rpm must be right for the best energy output. The ability to pedal smoothly and easily at such a high rate can be acquired through long practice. This naturally means long periods pedalling a small gear (say 42 × 17 or 18). Top class riders spend the whole winter on such small gears, putting in between 1000 and 5000km before they go to their training camp. High intensity training comes only later. In order to get good pedal training some riders adopt a 'fixed wheel' — a hub without a freewheel. This means that while in motion the rider is constantly pedalling. The very mechanics of a fixed wheel require the pedalling action to be good, otherwise the style begins to deteriorate, and the rider will start to bounce on the saddle. Any road-racing bike can be converted to fixed wheel. You just put a single cog (say of 17 teeth) on the rear wheel and remove the gear mechanisms, then shorten the chain so it is taut when riding on the small chainwheel.

Once you have ridden 1000-1500km on the fixed wheel, you should at least have enough of a feel for the right pedalling style to be able to continue with a normal freewheel.

Good pedalling is an individual science which demands long and conscientious training. Only when you have mastered this ability to pedal without difficulty can you really call yourself a proper cyclist.

Gear restrictions applicable to schoolchildren and juniors

The importance of being able to pedal fast and smoothly is such that young riders must steer clear of big gears, for fear that their style will be spoiled.

The development of power can be hindered or even ruined by premature use of big gears. For this reason most national cycling federations impose gear restrictions on young riders, depending on their age and the type of racing undertaken.

The British Cycling Federation, which governs road and track racing, has laid down gear restrictions affecting young riders, with the aim of compelling them to learn fast pedalling in the early stages of their racing career.

Schoolboys and schoolgirls are limited to a maximum gear of 76.2 inches (6.083 metres), for instance 48 × 17 in circuit races. In track racing the upper limit is 81 inches (6.464 metres), for example 48 × 16 (see page 86). Juniors (and incidentally any senior riders competing against them) have an upper limit for road racing of 86.4 inches (6.896 metres), for example 48 × 15. In track races they are not restricted.

Riders are split into categories for all road and track racing, but there is quite a generous mixing of categories in events with the notable exception of schoolboys, who may only race against others of their category. Women can even race against men, and frequently do. The rider's category is decided on his or her age on the day of the event itself.

Age categories	
Schoolboys/girls	12–15
Juniors	16–17
Seniors	18 and over
Women	16 and over
Veterans	40 and over

Schoolboy racing.

Riding technique

When you have learned to sit properly on a racing machine, to develop a good style and to pedal easily and well, you must go on to improve your riding technique. There are certain basic principles you should know. In the course of time you must learn to master your machine in all kinds of situations. In cycling particularly, it is important to use your energy rationally and economically, as at the speeds involved you must overcome resistances not encountered in sports that involve only unaided strength.

Physical principles

The racing cyclist must overcome three resisting forces:

1. Rolling resistance ('drag')
2. Wind resistance
3. Gravity

When you are riding on the flat, only drag and wind resistance will bother you, but when you are climbing hills, gravity must also be mastered. You have to know what factors affect these various resisting forces, so you can take steps to minimize their effects. It will all serve to improve your performance in the long run.

Rolling resistance

There are several kinds of rolling resistance in play during cycling: friction of the turning pedals, friction on the bottom bracket bearings, friction of the chain, and the friction of the wheels on the road. The greatest drag is caused by the contact between the tyre tread and the road surface. Rolling resistance F_R depends on the following factors.

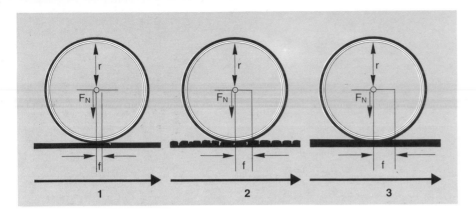

Rolling resistance relative to the contact surface of the tyre.
1. The tyre pressure is high enough, the road surface is smooth, contact surface *f* is small, and so is the rolling resistance.
2. The tyre pressure is too low, the road surface uneven. Contact surface *f* and rolling resistance increase.
3. Although the road surface is good and smooth, rolling resistance is still increased because the contact surface is enlarged because of too-low tyre pressure.

F_N = Normal force, consisting of the downward force exerted by the combined weight of the rider and machine.

r = Radius of the wheels.

f = Distance between the theoretical point where the tyre meets the road and the actual first point where the tyre touches.

So rolling resistance can be worked out using the following formula:

$$F_R = F_N \cdot \frac{f}{r}$$

From this formula the cyclist can deduce the following:

☐ The greater the combined weight of rider and machine, the greater the rolling resistance. So the rider and the machine should be as light as possible, to keep the drag down. There is no point in a light machine if the rider is overweight.

☐ The less the pressure in the tyre, the greater the contact area of the tyre on the road, and thus the greater the drag. Heavy tyres have a result similar to lighter low-pressure ones.

☐ On uneven roads the drag increases, for when the bike hits a pothole the effective tyre contact area increases.

☐ With higher tyre pressures the contact area decreases, and with it the drag. However, this can be disadvantageous in certain circumstances, for example in wet weather or slippery conditions, when you need good road contact. When climbing hills out of the saddle the back wheel can slide around, and on bad road surfaces an overinflated tyre can cause the wheel to jump about and so destroy the rider's rhythm.

☐ Rolling resistance increases if the wheel diameter is reduced. But most racing-cycle wheels have the same diameter, 27in (68.58cm).

Wind resistance
Wind resistance grows with speed. In road racing on flat courses, and in track races, this is the greatest resistance to be overcome.
Wind resistance F_L is influenced by the following factors:

A = The frontal area in square metres of the rider and machine (A = average width × height).

c_W = Wind resistance rating, the factor of the shape of the vehicle concerned. In the case of the cyclist himself, this means his aerodynamic posture and the surface texture of his race clothing.

Q = The density of the air, which on flat land at sea level is 1.23kg/m³, and at 2200m altitude (as in Mexico) is reduced to 1.0kg/m³.

v^2 = Square of the riding speed.

These values are used in the following formula:

$$F_L = A \cdot c_w \frac{Q}{2} \cdot v^2$$

From this we can work out the following principles:

☐ The smaller the frontal area of the rider, the smaller his wind resistance. A low position cuts to half the resistance of the normal leisure riding position.
☐ An aerodynamic position on the bicycle cuts down the wind resistance rating and consequently the wind resistance itself. A smooth and stylish riding style improves the streamlining.
☐ A smooth surface to the racing clothing, preferably lying as close to the body as possible, reduces the resistance.

☐ These factors are particularly relevant in sprints, track races, time trials and breakaway attempts, because wind resistance squares as speed increases.
☐ Record attempts, especially the world hour record, have a better chance at altitude, because the air density is less.

The **combined resistance F,** which the rider must overcome on flat roads, a dry asphalt surface and in calm conditions, is worked out from this equation:

$$F = F_R + F_L$$

Thus rolling resistance and wind resistance are added together.

So you can count on your best possible performance if you do everything to reduce the rolling and wind resistances. But there is still the telling factor that wind resistance increases as the square of the speed, and the relationship between increasing speed and increasing effort is shown here on a diagram.

The graph (see page 76) reveals two basic principles:

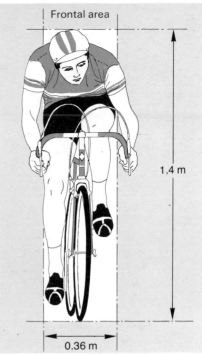

Frontal area of the machine and rider (in this case 0.5m²).

1. Effort P_R for rolling resistance F_R has a linear increase with speed v.
2. Effort P_L for wind resistance F_L shows a cubic increase with speed (thus v^3).

You can also see that until about 38 kilometres per hour wind resistance plays a smaller part than rolling resistance. From this point on, an increasing amount of effort must be expended to break through the increasing barrier of the wind. For example, at 40 kilometres per hour you have to put

75

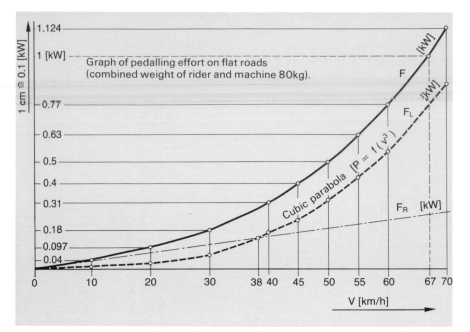

Graph of pedalling effort on flat roads (combined weight of rider and machine 80kg).

$1 \text{ cm} \stackrel{\wedge}{=} 0.1$ [kW]

Cubic parabola $[P = f(v^3)]$

F [kW]
F_L [kW]
F_R [kW]

V [km/h]

The force of gravity must be overcome when climbing hills, and adds to the rider's momentum on descents.

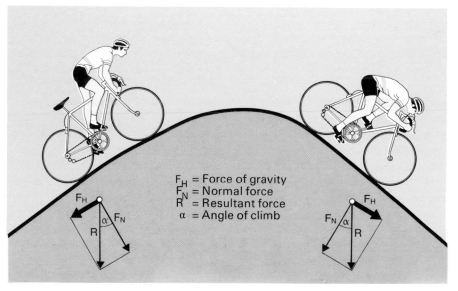

F_H = Force of gravity
F_N = Normal force
R = Resultant force
α = Angle of climb

out 0.31kW, equivalent to 0.426 horsepower. With an effort of 1.0kW, equalling 1.36 hp, you can reach a speed of 67 kilometres per hour — sprinting speed.

So you can see what considerable amounts of energy a rider must expend as riding speed increases. I should add as a comparison that the effective capacity of an untrained 20-year-old man is around 0.2kW, an effort which would bring him up to only 30 kilometres per hour, and only for a short time; an untrained person cannot keep up maximum effort for long. The average speeds in time trials are 40-45 kilometres per hour, sometimes even higher. In 100km team time trials they reach average speeds of 50 kilometres per hour.

Gravity

When you are going uphill, you have to overcome the force of gravity. This means you go more slowly. But it also means that wind resistance loses its great significance, so the rider can happily let his frontal area increase when he is climbing, and perhaps assume a more comfortable, if less aerodynamic, posture.

The force of gravity F_H consists of the following factors:

F_N = As before, the combined weight of rider and machine.

h = Difference in altitude.

l = Length of climb.

These factors combine in the following equation:

$$F_H = F_N \cdot \frac{h}{l}$$

The important results this yields are:

☐ The greater the climb, the greater the force of gravity.
☐ The greater the combined weight of rider and machine, the greater the force of gravity. Lighter riders have an advantage over heavier ones. Saving weight on the bicycle is more important on climbs than on the flat.
☐ On climbs an aerodynamic posture is less important than at higher speeds on the flat.

Here you can see a graph of what happens on a 12 per cent gradient (1 in 8) with a rider and machine together weighing

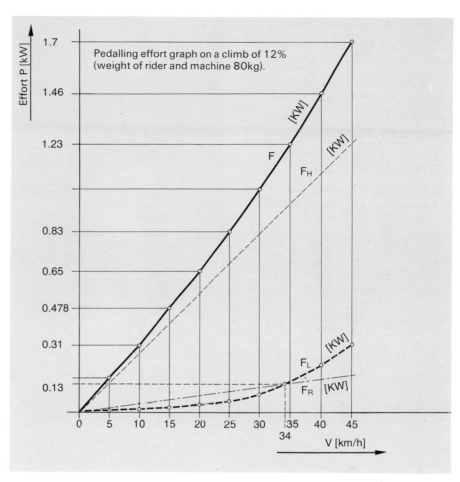

Pedalling effort graph on a climb of 12% (weight of rider and machine 80kg).

80kg. From the graph it is clear that a given rider who puts out 0.31kW, meaning a speed of 40 kilometres per hour on the flat, can only manage 10 kilometres per hour on a 12 per cent climb. The sprinter, who on the flat can put out 1kW in short bursts to produce 67 kilometres per hour, would manage a mere 30 kilometres per hour on the same climb. Thus you can see what

great effect gravity has on the possible performances of riders. On the other hand, the rider is free of the adverse forces of gravity when he is going downhill, and consequently can reach high speeds. Because of the increasing speed, wind resistance comes back into the reckoning, squaring as the speed grows. From these facts we can make the following observations

'Honking'. The body weight is over the straight leg, while the machine is pulled to the opposite side by arm and back strength. In this way the entire body can be set to work.

Riding positions for hills

Essentially there are four different positions for hill riding.

1. Standing on the pedals — 'honking'.
2. In the saddle, holding the tops of the handlebars.
3. In the saddle, holding the brake hoods.
4. The descending position.

Climbing hills means low speed and low wind resistance. The three first positions are fine. Because of the high speed of descents, the wind resistance is great and the position adopted should be as low and aerodynamic as possible.

'Honking'

This style of climbing allows the athletic potential of the whole body to be brought into play. Its essence is in skilfully using your body weight to employ as little effort as possible. The body weight acts downward on the straight leg, making the arms and body exert a pull on the handlebars to slant the bike sideways in the other direction, the torso always staying vertical. For example, when the left leg is

about **going downhill**:

☐ The greater the gradient, the greater the effect of gravity.

☐ The greater the weight of the rider, the greater his descending speed.

☐ An aerodynamic posture minimizes wind resistance on high-speed descents.

If one could manage to come down that 12 per cent hill unobstructed, without bends or other hazards to worry about, a 70kg rider with a 10kg bike would reach a speed of 97 kilometres per hour without even having to pedal. In fact, speeds of 80 kilometres per hour and above are rarely reached on descents.

straight, then the right hand is pushing the handlebars downward, the left hand pulling upward at the same time, the machine tilting to the right. You grip the handlebars either by the brake levers or by the drops. This style of riding is mostly used on steep gradients, but also for breakaway attempts and other sharp accelerations. Hill specialists, the climbers, can manage long sections using the 'honking' style.

Some such climbing experts, like Spain's Federico Bahamontes, also known as the 'Eagle of Toledo', would regularly change from 'honking' to a sitting position during long ascents. Bahamontes would do 12 pedal revs 'honking', then 12 in turn sitting down, throughout the whole climb. The use of the 'honking' style shows how important it is for a rider to have sturdy arms, back and upper body muscles.

While 'honking', you must take care that the body weight is properly used. Adopt too far forward a posture and the back wheel will tend to move about. If the centre of gravity is too far back, you cannot use your body weight properly, and cannot bring

Climbing position holding the brake lever hoods.

Climbing position holding the tops.

into play the upper body and arm muscles as well as possible. 'Honking' should be a distinct part of your training programme; this style is often very valuable in decisive phases of a race, so it has to be mastered.

Climbing with your hands on the tops of the handlebars
This position is most usual on long climbs. You sit well back in the saddle and pay attention to lifting the toes as you pass the top dead centre point of the revolution.

Climbing with hands on the brake lever hoods
This position is recommended on

medium-length climbs. It allows you to pedal with maximum power, making the best use of arm, torso and leg muscles. As you are not bent over sharply, your breathing isn't hindered. Another point is that it is easy to switch to the 'honking' style if you have to tackle a steeper gradient or accelerate suddenly.

Going downhill
After the mighty effort that brings you over the crest of a hill, you put in the big gear and assume your most aerodynamic posture. You bend low over the bars, keeping your elbows tucked in and your knees close to the frame. The cranks and your feet

should be horizontal. Your head should be nicely tucked in, but lifted enough to see what is coming. On descents you can reach and maintain high speeds, thanks to the forces of gravity, which are now on your side. Speeds of 80 kilometres per hour and more are possible, but you must still concentrate even though you are no longer making maximum physical effort. You have to watch out for hazards and rough sections of road. You must take every corner perfectly, assessing your speed against the tightness of any bends, to hold the best line.

Keep your leg muscles loose, especially on long descents, so

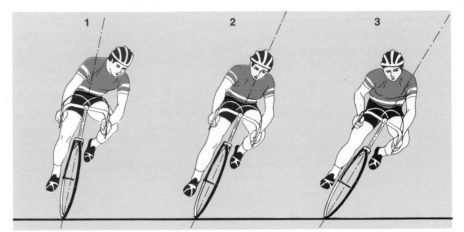

Riding position on a bend. In principle there are three ways to counter centrifugal force:
1. The body is leaned towards the inside of the bend, but the bike is not leaned as far.
2. Body and machine are both leaned into the bend at the same angle.
3. The machine is leaned into the bend but the upper body is either upright or even leaned slightly the other way.

Aerodynamic descending position.

you don't risk cramp. From time to time you can stretch one leg or the other, easily rocking the pedals back and forward. These movements should stop your muscles stiffening up or getting too cold, for at high speed it is all too easy to get the muscles and joints chilled, which is dangerous. Otherwise you can warm up your muscles nicely when you reach flat ground, with a session of fast pedalling on lower gears.

Cornering

Cornering technique is very important, and at high speeds can be vital. If you go into a corner too fast, you can easily leave the road. You can also come to grief if your pedal touches the ground on the inside of the bend. But beware of braking too hard, for you can lose valuable speed that way. It's also dangerous to brake at the wrong moment.

The idea is to go through each bend at its maximum speed. The following factors are important when considering centrifugal force.

m = mass, measured in kilograms.

r = radius of the bend.

w = cornering speed.

Centrifugal force F_Z links the above factors this way:

$$F_Z = m \cdot r \cdot w^2$$

From this formula we can learn the following:

☐ Centrifugal force increases as does the combined weight of rider and machine.
☐ The force which tends to pull the rider towards the outside of the bend is greater as the radius of the curve lessens. Centrifugal force increases as the square of the speed.
☐ You can counter the tendency to drift out on a bend by leaning bike and body weight into the bend.
☐ You can increase this counteracting force by leaning your body into the

wind and raising your inner knee (see picture).
☐ The maximum amount you can lean on dry asphalt is about 73°, perhaps 80° on tarmacadam. Any steeper angle could make the bike skid from underneath its rider.
☐ It is good to put more weight on the rear wheel when cornering, by sliding back on the saddle.
☐ You should follow a riding line on the bend that effectively increases its radius.

Riding position on a bend: machine and body are leaning into the bend, with the inside pedal raised.

Riding line on bends. The effective radius of the bend is increased, and thus sideways force reduced.

□ If you have to brake, do it before the bend, not while you are actually cornering.
□ Since the tendency to drift works principally on the tyres, make sure they are well stuck on.

On descents you should remember that tyres at very high pressure have greatly decreased rolling resistance, especially if the road is wet or covered in loose sand. Also, don't use your most aggressive cornering technique on blind bends, never cutting corners unless you are racing on closed roads. With this exception, always make allowances for traffic and road safety, adjusting your speed to the relative road conditions. If you are racing, and find yourself in a group, try to get in front for the corners, so you can choose your ideal line. If this isn't possible, then try to keep to the inside of the bend. On the outside you can be brought down by a skidding rider.

Wheel-following

In working out wind resistance, we saw that it squares with increasing speed. But you can make considerable reductions in wind resistance if you make use of the 'wind shadow' of the leading rider. In order to do this, you must ride closely behind, something like 5 or 10cm behind his rear tyre. You should, however, ride slightly to the side, so that you don't crash if the leading rider suddenly brakes. Following a wheel in this way demands concentration and skill, and both should be improved upon in training. To stop your concentration lapsing, you can let your eye wander a little: from the rear tyre to his freewheel, his legs, his back, and then returning to the rear tyre.

You place yourself behind according to the wind direction. In a sidewind coming from the right, you ride slightly to the left of the rider in front, and in a sidewind from the left you ride to his right, yet still behind. In a headwind you ride virtually behind. As every rider will seek this ideal position, it is normal for 'echelons' to form (see photo and diagram). Under ordinary traffic conditions this is not really possible, but you can ride slightly to one side. In races, cyclists share the work against wind resistance, the front man swinging off and drifting to the back of the string of riders, moving gradually sideways out of the wind as he does so, until he reaches the back of the line, then starting to move up again as others take their turns in front. Doing 'bit and bit', as this work-sharing technique is called, works well on narrow roads, where true echelons are not possible. The motion of the group is that of a continually revolving circle or chain.

Slipstreaming, demonstrated by Dietrich Thurau and Gregor Braun.

Riders' turns at the front of such a working group tend to be shorter as the headwind increases. Weaker riders also take shorter turns at the front. All this presupposes that members of such a group are really doing their best to share the work. Sometimes, unsportingly, riders do not take their turns at the front, but when they come to the lead swing straight off again, perhaps with the aim of saving themselves for the finishing sprint.

Echelon.

Slipstreaming.

Echelon riding: with the wind from the left, the echelon is to the right.

Swinging off and falling to the back of the echelon.

Dealing with obstacles

At relatively high riding speeds you should keep a careful eye on road surfaces and direction. But there are always unforeseen obstacles to be tackled, such as potholes, ramps, gutters, ruts (and, on the Continent, tramlines) and so on. In such situations it is important not to lose control of the machine. So I recommend that in training you practise dealing with obstacles. Cross tramlines diagonally, and use the same technique for wide gutters or ditches. Take a direct line through short, rough or muddy sections. Bear in mind that on wet, muddy or oily surfaces your grip is reduced, especially on tight

Tackling obstacles: crossing a ditch. 1 is right, 2 is wrong.

bends. If confronted by potholes, narrow ditches, rocks or tree-roots, you had best lift the front wheel, or jump the whole bike.

With a sudden backward movement of your body and a pull on the bars, you can lift the front wheel 40–50cm off the ground. The best way of practising this is by jumping up over a kerbstone. You can even lift your back wheel, by leaning the body forward over the bars, coming off the saddle and jerking up with both feet (strapped in, of course) at the same time. By performing a combination of these two manoeuvres, you can jump obstacles as much as 1.5–2m across, lifting the bike 12–30cm off the ground. Jumping the bike is performed in the following manner (see pictures 1–3). Keeping the cranks horizontal, get out of the saddle until your legs are stretched. Just before the obstacle you slightly bend your knees and then pull up on the handlebars and up with both feet. The higher the obstacle, the more energetically you must do this. Of course your feet should be tightly strapped in, otherwise they will come out of the toe-clips. You must keep a

firm grip on the handlebars, and the bars should be held quite straight, as otherwise you could crash on landing; if you land diagonally, the tyres could be torn off.

Naturally, in training you should not try out such jumps at high speed; start at walking pace. Better to work first on lifting the front wheel; when you have mastered this you can proceed to tackle short jumps. All this is part of really advanced riding technique. By improving your control of the machine you become one with it, and know that you can react quickly to unforeseen obstacles and circumstances. In races you can even find yourself jumping over fallen riders. Knowing instinctively that you can overcome such obstacles, you will ride in a more relaxed fashion.

Choosing the right gear

Gearing and gear ratios depend on the relationship between the front and rear parts of the transmission system, and on a bicycle they are subject to certain physical laws relating to chain drive.

The correct use of gearing on a bicycle depends on the most economic use of strength, speed and stamina. In early cycling history you selected your gear on the direct-drive High Bicycle or Penny-Farthing by choosing the right size of front wheel. From

this modest beginning has developed the modern 12-speed gearing. With the help of a 5- or 6-speed freewheel and a double chainwheel you can theoretically have 10 or 12 different gear ratios. As you are bound to lose a couple through bad chain lines, this leaves 8 to 10 combinations. Gearing and pedalling are influenced by the following factors:

☐ Size of the chainwheel
☐ Size of the sprocket
☐ Length of the cranks
☐ Diameter of the driven wheel

Gearing: the greater the gear, the greater the distance travelled with one pedal revolution, but also the greater the energy expended.

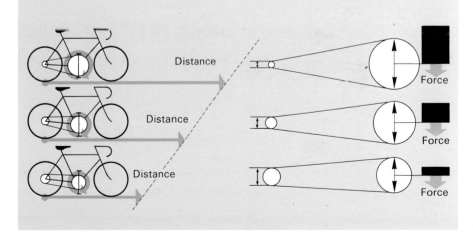

Racing bikes have wheels of a nominal 27 in (68.58 cm). Even countries using decimal measurements express gear ratios in inches, a throwback to the early days of the bicycle when the front driving wheel was measured in inches. Since neither crank length nor wheel size are subject to great change, the essential factors are thus the chainwheel and sprocket sizes. Using these factors, you can reach a measurement in inches or in metres.

Measurement in inches

Normally gear ratios are given in inches, since this method has been long adopted by cyclists. The formula uses the following:

d = diameter of the driving wheel in inches (usually 27)
z_1 = number of teeth on the chainwheel
z_2 = number of teeth on the sprocket

Your gear in inches is calculated as
$$\frac{z_1 \times d}{z_2}$$

For example, if you have a chainwheel with 53 teeth, and a rear sprocket of 16, then you have a gear of:

$$\frac{53 \times 27}{16} = 89.44\,in$$

Measurement in metres

This measurement gives the distance travelled with one pedal revolution. It is seldom used in Britain or Germany, but widely used in France. In fact, for many people this method is a more logical way. It uses the following factors:

u = circumference of the rear wheel

This is discovered from diameter × 3.14 (π). On a 27 in wheel it is $27 \times 2.54 \times 3.14 = 215.3\,cm$. Round this off to 215 cm or 2.15 m.

z_1 = number of teeth on the chainwheel
z_2 = number of teeth on the rear sprocket

These factors are combined as follows:

$$\text{Gear (in metres)} = \frac{z_1 \times u}{z_2}$$

Using the same example as above, we get the following distance travelled per pedal revolution:

$$\frac{53 \times 2.15}{16} = 7.12$$

This is equivalent to a gear ratio of 89.44 in. On the table of metric values the figure will be lower than 7.12 m, since in practice, because the tyre is not solid, it will be somewhat flattened, so that a 27 in wheel is rated at 26.76 in. When talking of gear ratios, the metric value is rarely used. You simply say you are riding 89.44 (or simply 89) or riding a 53 × 16.

Since working out each gear ratio, in inches or metres, is a fussy business, there are helpful tables which do the work for you. These tables are especially useful when you are working out a range of gears, and don't want to have any duplication. A gear of 51 × 17 is the equivalent of 42 × 14. With our recommended standard gear range of 53/42 × 13, 14, 15, 17, 19, 21, you have the

following table of results.

Sprocket teeth	Chainwheel 42	43	44	45	46	47	48	49	50	51	52	53	54	55	Gear table in inches 56
12	94.5	96.8	99.0	101.3	103.5	105.8	108.0	110.3	112.5	114.8	117.0	119.3	121.5	123.8	126.0
13	87.2	89.3	91.4	93.4	95.4	97.5	98.8	101.8	103.8	105.8	108.1	110.0	112.1	114.2	116.3
14	81.0	82.9	84.9	86.8	88.7	90.6	92.5	94.5	96.4	98.4	100.3	102.2	104.2	106.0	107.3
15	75.6	77.4	79.2	81.0	82.8	84.6	86.4	88.2	90.0	91.8	93.6	95.4	97.2	99.0	100.8
16	70.9	72.5	74.3	76.0	77.6	79.3	81.0	82.7	84.4	86.1	87.8	89.5	91.2	92.8	94.5
17	66.7	68.3	69.9	71.5	73.0	74.6	76.2	77.8	79.4	81.0	82.6	84.2	85.6	87.3	88.9
18	63.0	64.5	66.0	67.5	69.0	70.5	72.0	73.5	75.0	76.5	78.0	79.5	81.0	82.5	84.0
19	59.7	61.1	62.5	64.0	65.4	66.8	68.2	69.6	71.1	72.5	73.9	75.4	76.7	78.0	79.4
20	56.7	58.1	59.4	60.8	62.1	63.5	64.8	66.2	67.5	68.9	70.2	71.6	72.8	74.2	75.6
21	54.0	55.3	56.6	57.9	59.1	60.4	61.7	63.0	64.3	65.6	66.9	68.1	69.4	70.5	72.0
22	51.5	52.8	54.0	55.2	56.5	57.7	58.9	60.1	61.4	62.6	63.8	65.0	66.3	67.5	68.7
23	49.3	50.5	51.7	52.8	54.0	55.2	56.3	57.5	58.7	59.9	61.0	62.2	63.3	64.5	65.7
24	47.3	48.4	49.5	50.6	51.8	52.9	54.0	55.1	56.3	57.4	58.5	59.2	60.0	61.8	63.0
25	45.4	46.4	47.5	48.6	49.7	50.8	51.8	52.9	54.0	55.1	56.2	57.4	58.3	59.4	60.4
26	43.6	44.6	45.7	46.7	47.8	48.8	49.8	50.9	51.9	52.9	54.0	55.0	56.1	57.1	58.1

Sprocket teeth	Chainwheel 42	43	44	45	46	47	48	49	50	51	52	53	54	55	Gear table in metres 56
12	7.47	7.65	7.83	8.01	8.18	8.36	8.54	8.72	8.90	9.07	9.25	9.43	9.61	9.79	9.97
13	6.90	7.06	7.23	7.39	7.55	7.72	7.88	8.05	8.21	8.38	8.54	8.70	8.87	9.03	9.20
14	6.40	6.56	6.71	6.86	7.01	7.17	7.32	7.47	7.63	7.78	7.93	8.08	8.23	8.39	8.54
15	5.98	6.12	6.26	6.40	6.55	6.69	6.83	6.97	7.12	7.26	7.40	7.54	7.69	7.83	7.97
16	5.60	5.74	5.87	6.00	6.14	6.27	6.40	6.54	6.67	6.81	6.94	7.07	7.20	7.34	7.47
17	5.27	5.40	5.52	5.65	5.78	5.90	6.03	6.15	6.28	6.40	6.53	6.66	6.78	6.91	7.03
18	4.98	5.10	5.22	5.34	5.45	5.57	5.69	5.81	5.93	6.05	6.17	6.29	6.40	6.52	6.64
19	4.72	4.83	4.94	5.05	5.17	5.28	5.39	5.50	5.62	5.73	5.84	5.95	6.07	6.18	6.29
20	4.48	4.59	4.70	4.80	4.91	5.02	5.12	5.23	5.34	5.44	5.55	5.66	5.76	5.87	5.98
21	4.27	4.37	4.47	4.57	4.67	4.78	4.88	4.98	5.08	5.18	5.29	5.39	5.49	5.59	5.69
22	4.07	4.17	4.27	4.37	4.46	4.56	4.66	4.75	4.85	4.95	5.04	5.14	5.24	5.34	5.43
23	3.90	3.99	4.08	4.18	4.27	4.36	4.45	4.55	4.64	4.73	4.83	4.92	5.01	5.10	5.20
24	3.73	3.82	3.91	4.00	4.09	4.18	4.27	4.36	4.45	4.54	4.62	4.71	4.80	4.89	4.98
25	3.58	3.67	3.76	3.84	3.93	4.01	4.10	4.18	4.27	4.35	4.44	4.52	4.61	4.69	4.78
26	3.45	3.53	3.61	3.69	3.78	3.86	3.94	4.02	4.10	4.19	4.27	4.35	4.43	4.51	4.60

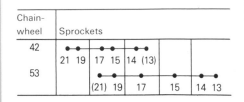

Chainwheel	Sprockets				
42	21 19	17 15 14 (13)			
53	(21) 19	17	15	14 13	

If we sort these gears out, you have the following progression from lowest gear to highest:

1. 42 × 21
2. 42 × 19
3. 42 × 17
4. 42 × 15. This ratio is virtually the same as 53 × 19, but has a much better chain-line, so is used for preference.
5. 42 × 14
6. 53 × 17. For short climbs you can change down from this gear to a 53 × 19, since it can be done more quickly than changing to 42 × 14. But on longer climbs, change to 42 × 14 because of the better chain-line.
7. 53 × 15
8. 53 × 14
9. 53 × 13

The gear you choose depends on several circumstances and situations.

- The individual's talents (stamina, speed, power)
- Terrain (hills, mountains, flat, descents)
- Wind conditions (headwind, tailwind)
- Road surface (macadam, cobbles, potholes, rough roads)
- The tactical situation of the race (breakaway, echelon, bunch, prime sprint, finishing sprint, time trial, team time trial and so on)

Choosing the right gear is thus related to your own physical state, the external conditions, and the state of the race. Your gear choice must suit all three at once, to give the right pedalling rate and to conserve your energy until thc right momont. Using the formula that work = force × distance, it follows that if work stays constant, then force will be greater if distance (that is, the distance covered by the revolving pedals) is reduced. Conversely, if work remains constant, the force used will be lessened if the number of revolutions is increased. For every situation there is an optimal relationship between force and distance. In cycling terms, this is between power input and pedalling speed.

Using big gears (90–112in) the power input is very high, the pedalling speed relatively low. Per revolution the rider covers between 7.13 and 8.94m, the gear ratio between 53 × 16 and 54 × 13. You can only learn to handle such big gears after years of training, and stay away from them in your early years. Gears of this order are primarily used in time trials, and seldom in road and track races.

With middle-range gears (70–88in) your power input is medium, and so is your pedalling rate, with 5.6 to 7.0m covered per revolution, the ratios lying between 42 × 16 and 52 × 16. Medium gears are used in racing and training.

With low gears (below 70) pedalling rate takes a primary role, since power input is low. Using low gears you can train for stamina and speed. Each pedal revolution means a distance of 5.60m or less, and the ratio is below 42 × 16. Low gears are used in winter and spring to rediscover good fast pedalling and to develop stamina. You also use small gears during the recovery phases of interval training.

Different properties of similar gear ratios

As you can see from the gear tables, you can get the same gear ratio by many different combinations of chainwheels and sprockets. For example, an 81in gear (6.46m) can be obtained by using 42 × 14, 45 × 15, 48 × 16, 51 × 17 or 54 × 18. But don't run away with the idea that it doesn't matter which combination you choose.

Faced with such a choice, you should lean towards the combination with the greatest total number of chainwheel and sprocket teeth, for several reasons:

- Better distribution of power over the larger number of teeth.
- Because of this distribution, the tangential forces acting on chain, freewheel sprocket and hub are lessened.
- Lower torsional stress on the frame.

□ A more flexible and smoother pedalling action.

But combinations with high tooth totals have disadvantages too:

□ Possible need for a longer chain.

□ Increased weight of the transmission.

□ Starting and attacking efforts are slower and weaker.

Of course it follows that these advantages and disadvantages are reversed when you use low-tooth combinations. But weighing one against the other, you should go for the high-tooth combinations in time trials and long events over flattish terrain. In hilly terrain, or in events with sudden changes of tempo, depending on the ability to move suddenly into high speed, you are better to choose low-tooth combinations. A good example is in track racing, with a gear of 92in. In pursuiting, which calls for a pretty constant speed, you achieve this gear with 51 × 15. In sprints, where sudden acceleration is vital, you would go for 48 × 14.

Optimal pedalling rate

The 'best' pedalling rate has always been a moot point. Research in laboratories does not agree with the practical tests on, and the preferences of, actual racing cyclists. Riders seem to choose, for their training and racing, pedalling rates which are apparently uneconomical from the standpoint of energy use. If you were to test the average person or a poorly trained cyclist on a bicycle ergometer, you would get totally different results on the same work-load. For each graduated work-load there is an optimal pedalling rate which lies between 40 and 70rpm. Above and below these limits, relative energy output is higher.

However, there is a tendency to recognize that at high levels of efforts, and with increased fitness, a higher pedalling rate could indeed be more economic. For a well-trained cyclist the above rates are far too low, and would be unthinkable in a race. For the same racing speed and effort, a better-trained cyclist will choose to pedal faster, while the worse-trained athlete will instead resort to bigger and bigger gears,

and consequent lower pedalling speed. You can resolve these facts and practical conclusions from experience into two basic statements:

□ High level of fitness = high pedalling rate
□ Low level of fitness = low pedalling rate

At first sight this would seem to support the view that lower pedalling rates are more economic after all. Could it not be that the strong rider is able to squander his excess energy on faster pedalling, while the weaker rider is miserly with his available energy? In fact it isn't so, for in choosing the lower pedalling rate, a rider's performance decreases. Probably the most illuminating example of the relationship between pedalling speed and performance is the world hour record. A record aspirant rides for 60 minutes and the distance covered is measured. This is reckoned to be the toughest stamina test for a racing cyclist. The table on page 92 shows details of the record rides to date, with the distances covered, gears used, and average rpm.

Eddy Merckx, one of the
most successful riders of
all time.

From this table you can see two things:

- The world record is not beaten by using very big gears
- Riders have been virtually unanimous in their pedalling rate, which has varied over 30 years between 103 and 108rpm.

Of course you have to accept that a world record can only be set up in the best and most favourable conditions. And it would be illogical to think that successful record riders had deliberately chosen gear ratios that did not suit them. Therefore the optimal pedalling rate for a well-trained rider would lie, as previously indicated, somewhat over 100rpm.

In track races, and above all in sprinting, even higher pedalling rates are common, between 120 and 150rpm.

The reason for all this lies in the **muscle fibre constitution** of the leg muscles, which change in a certain way as a result of cycle training. Each muscle is made up of millions of muscle fibres, which fall into three separate types.

1. **Red, slow-twitch muscle fibres.** Their red colour comes from their high content of red muscle pigment (myoglobin) which, just like the red blood pigment (haemoglobin), is concerned with the use of oxygen. Oxygen is better transformed into energy by these fibres. The energy-producing reaction takes place in certain cells (mitochondria) as oxygen is used up (aerobic effort). The build-up of lactic acid, which happens if there is a lack of oxygen ('oxygen debt'), is low. As in long-term effort the consumption of both fat and carbohydrates plays a role, these muscle fibres contain fat and carbohydrate (muscle glycogen) as energy sources. As these muscle fibres contract only comparatively slowly, they are also called slow-twitch fibres. These red fibres are characteristically very resistant to fatigue, and thus they are found abundantly in riders with stamina.

2. **White, fast-twitch muscle fibres.** Their content of red muscle pigment is lower, and hence their ability to utilize oxygen is less. But in contrast to red fibres they can contract much more quickly, and for this reason are known as fast-twitch fibres. For rapid, explosive efforts they demand energy at such a rate that the body cannot keep up with the demand for oxygen, thus the energy reaction must take place without it (anaerobically), creating a lot of lactic acid. Their ability to produce energy through the utilization of oxygen (aerobic reaction) is lower, hence they tire more quickly under long efforts.

Rider	Year	Distance (km)	Gear	Average rpm
Coppi	1942	45.840	52 × 15	105.4
Anquetil	1956	46.169	52 × 15	105.9
Baldini	1956	46.393	52 × 15	106.6
Rivière	1957	46.923	52 × 15	107.9
Rivière	1958	47.347	53 × 15	106.8
Bracke	1967	48.093	54 × 15	104.2
Ritter	1972	48.634	54 × 15	105.4
Merckx	1972	49.431	52 × 14	103.9

3. Intermediate type muscle fibres. These occupy a middle position between the characteristics of red and white fibres.

Until recently it was believed that one's ratio of muscle fibre types was inborn, and thus immutable. It was felt that the only way an athlete could better adapt himself to a particular type of effort was by increasing the cross-sectional area of the important fibres — but this could be done only to a limited extent. This would mean that whoever was born with a greater proportion of fast-twitch fibres would be a sprinter, and whoever had more slow-twitch fibres would be a long-distance athlete. Now, however, we are discovering that practically everyone has an unexpected potential for stamina. It has been discovered in experiments with animals that by passing an appropriate electrical stimulus through it a slow-twitch fibre could become a fast-twitch fibre, and vice versa. If you also exchanged the nerves to these fibres, then the fibre properties would alter correspondingly. It would seem therefore that the stimulus or the nerve provision is

A road rider's legs are slim and lean.

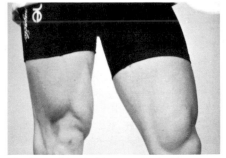
The legs of track riders, particularly sprinters, are more heavily muscled.

more important than the actual fibre.

Although results of animal tests don't always apply to humans, these have indicated sufficiently clearly that with the right training it should be possible to turn slow-twitch fibres into fast, and fast-twitch fibres into slow, at least within limits. This would also hold good for fibres of the intermediate type. Otherwise it would not be possible for world-class endurance athletes to have 70 to 90 per cent slow-twitch fibres, or world-class sprinters to have a similar level of fast-twitch fibres; for at birth they could have had no more than 50 to 60 per cent, the rest being provided by the right kind of training.

Road-racing cyclists, and those of any cycling discipline which demands a high level of stamina, need a large percentage of red, slow-twitch fibres in the appropriate muscles. The power capacity of these muscle fibres is lower, however, so that for a given work output the distance must be increased — by increasing the pedalling speed. Conversely, track riders, and above all sprinters, need a musculature chiefly made up of white, fast-twitch fibres. But the explosive energy release which results can only be of use in bursts of rapid activity. Exertion worsens the blood supply, so sheer strength should be used as sparingly as possible. Instead, a higher pedalling rate is once again indicated. It can take several years to build up the ability to maintain a high pedalling rate over a long period, as this makes special demands on the nervous system supplying the muscles, and this in turn can be developed only slowly. Nerves and muscle fibres act virtually as a unit (a so-called neuro-muscular unit).

This also explains why an exhausted rider, or one who has trained badly, cannot hold a high pedalling rate, because the tired nervous system cannot pass on the stimuli to the muscle groups as quickly as can the system of a fresh or well-trained rider.

Summary

Whether you ride professionally or just as a hobby, you should train at maximum pedalling rate on low gears. Only this way can you build up the right constitution of muscle fibres. As you get fitter, so you can increase the pedalling speed. Eventually you should have no trouble reaching around 120rpm. Then when things get serious, in races, it will be easier to cope with the lower pedalling rate of around 100rpm for longer periods.

For track riders, especially sprinters, it is different. They will increase the number of white fibres (fast-twitch) by sprints and other methods of power training. From experience we know that it takes longer to build up slow-twitch fibres for endurance than fast-twitch fibres for sudden effort. This is reflected in training programmes; the training of sprinters is only some 20 per cent power-oriented, with some 80 per cent directed towards stamina.

Technique, training and talent are interwoven in human performance.

The four essentials of a good racing cyclist

All of this, then, establishes these four fundamental requirements for a cyclist:

☐ Good riding position.
☐ An easy riding style.
☐ Mastery of the art of pedalling.
☐ The ability to sustain a fast pedalling rate over a long period.

These essentials are worth striving for, even by the average rider. The pleasure you derive from cycle racing, and the performance you achieve, will be increased by developing these essentials.

The 'human machine'

Bicycle and cyclist are two different machines which must collaborate as fully as possible to reach a high level of performance. The one machine, the bicycle, is made of metal, rubber and leather; the other, the man, is made of cells, tissues and organs. You can only make two machines function as one if you know and understand them both. So the cyclist should be every bit as familiar with the workings of his body as he is with the technical operations of his racing bicycle. The construction and functioning of the human body can only be briefly described here. But it is a great advantage if, during the development of his career, a sportsman can perfect his knowledge in this area. For only in understanding the construction of the body can a racing cyclist appreciate the various training methods and nutritional principles, and so apply these to improve his performance. To start with, let us take a short excursion into the field of physiology.

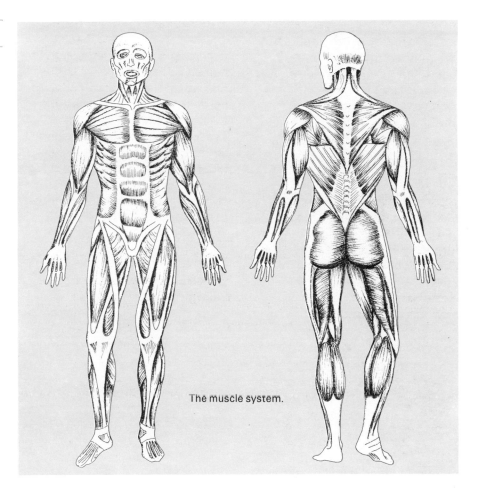

The muscle system.

Mitochondria — powerhouse of the cells

The cells of the human body are composed of a nucleus, cytoplasm, the cell membrane, and various organelles, the most important of which include the mitochondria.

In the mitochondria the energy-delivering processes take place. Through stamina training the various muscular-skeletal systems increase the number and size of the mitochondria according to the demands placed on them.

Mitochondria are rod-like in shape, with an outer and inner membrane bearing the various enzymes essential for energy processes. The nutrients — carbohydrates, fats and proteins — are held separately within the cell body, but outside the mitochondria, ready to be called in for the provision of energy, which takes place inside the mitochondria. In this cell powerhouse the nutrients are broken down into carbon dioxide and water. The greater part of the energy released goes into the respiratory system, where finally the hydrogen delivered from the nutrients combines with the oxygen delivered by the bloodstream. The energy created is stored in the form of energy-rich phosphates (ATP and creatin phosphate). Energy supply and demand are balanced by a special system. In this way mitochondria act as the fundamental creators of physical stamina.

The basics of motor fitness

Organs and organ systems of the human body are subject, in the fulfilling of their functions, to certain laws of nature common to all living things.

The following rule applies: the structure and performance of an organ or organ system is decided by its inherited characteristics, and from the quality and quantity of its exercise.

The more intensively, within fixed physiological limits, an organ is exercised, the better it will be suited to the required performance.

In principle, one can define the following **five main characteristics of movement:**

1. Co-ordination (technique)

2. Flexibility (suppleness)

3. Strength

4. Speed

5. Endurance or stamina

By **co-ordination** or technique we mean the cooperation of the central nervous system and the muscular-skeletal system within a certain desired range of movements.

By **flexibility** or suppleness we mean the capability of a range of movement at will over one or several joints. This is made possible by the combination of various muscle groups, the agonists and antagonists to a given movement.

Considering **strength,** one should differentiate between static strength, dynamic strength, and power. Static strength is applied at will against a fixed resistance. Dynamic strength is that whose release is in a desired movement. Finally, power is the amount of dynamic strength which can be applied at a given moment.

Speed comes from four factors, namely reaction time, which is the elapsed time from a given signal until the beginning of a conscious movement; the rapidity of a movement, the possible frequency of the movement in a given time, and the attained forward speed. Under the heading of speed one should distinguish between basic speed and sustained speed, the latter being more subject to improvement through training.

By **endurance** or stamina we mean the ability to sustain a given level of effort over the longest possible period. Part of stamina is being able to resist the onset of fatigue. Under this heading one should distinguish between aerobic and anaerobic endurance, that is, whether the effort is sustained with or without adequate oxygen supplies. The former is the province of the long-distance athlete, while the latter is that of the short-distance specialist.

In order to reach a completely exhausted state in the physical sense, it must be assumed that there is the right mental stimulus — **motivation.**

The ability to perform is through awareness, through positive motivation.

Effects of cycle sport on the body

In the course of time, the body adjusts itself to the demands which cycle sport places upon it. The power output of a track sprinter demands, above all, the ability to produce anaerobic effort, drawing on energy-rich phosphates and glycogen in an anaerobic state. Through exercising the muscles for strength and speed, the white, fast-twitch fibres are formed and developed for a high anaerobic capacity. The circulation system of the heart should not be as strongly developed as with a road rider, since the priority is for anaerobic energy, and thus the better oxygen transport system needed for aerobic effort is not as important. In addition, the track sprinter can have a greater body-weight, for maximal oxygen uptake per kilogram of body-weight is not so important as with a road rider. High body-weight is also necessary for the all-important bursts of speed in sprinting.

The track rider more oriented towards stamina (kilometre time-trial rider, pursuiter, tandemist) will adopt an intermediate solution between that of the sprinter and that of the roadman. Six-day riders and motor-paced riders are real endurance cyclists, who are still drawn from the ranks of trackmen. Good pursuiters are frequently good road riders. A roadman must develop the ability to produce a high level of effort over a longer period. His energy potential is almost exclusively aerobic, burning up available stores of carbohydrates and fats. As his endurance training condition improves, so the number of red, slow-twitch muscle fibres increases. At the same level of effort as an untrained rider, the stamina-trained rider is able to answer more of his energy demands by burning up fats. This means that he still has reserves of carbohydrates for urgent needs, such as a prime sprint, breakaway effort or finishing sprint.

It is a good sign in a road rider if he is able to use fat stores for energy at an ever-increasing level of effort. Once he starts to tap his carbohydrate stores, fatigue begins to take effect. The longer he can stave off fatigue, the better his stamina training has been.

The cardio-vascular circulation as oxygen transport system

With the increase in chemical changes because of endurance efforts, the organism places greater demands for oxygen, especially at the working sites — the muscles directly involved in the exercise.

For this reason the body must ensure that the maximum amount of oxygen can be transported to the cells. This comes about through an improved blood supply to the working muscle groups, through an increase in the size of the heart, and through the development of the lungs. The combined result is that the body works more efficiently.

It is simply able to take up more oxygen, which is the biological measure of how well it is suited to endurance efforts. Certainly this measurement, maximum oxygen uptake, is subject to the ageing process, and reduces with passing years. But by regular endurance training this ability can be improved, and maintained to a good age. Cycle racing is one of the sports which develops the ability to take up oxygen. Related to body weight, this maximal oxygen uptake (aerobic capacity) is the most important way of assessing an athlete's potential for endurance effort. In the untrained mature man it normally lies between 35 and 45 litres of oxygen per minute for each kilogram of body weight. Through stamina training this value can be built up to around 80.

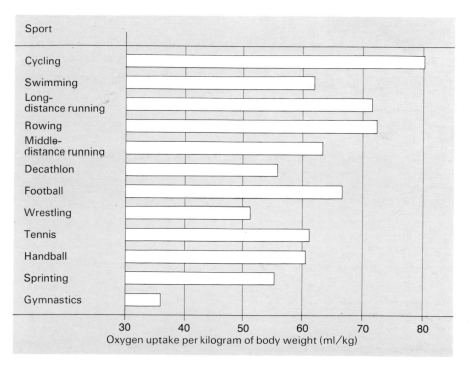

Sport and heart size

Heart of an untrained person
(about 600–700cc)

Heart of the trained athlete
(1000–1400cc)

Oxygen uptake per kilogram of body weight (ml/kg)

The increase in the volume of the heart chambers is only a second adaptation to the necessity of meeting the body's increased oxygen demands. Sportsmen with the greatest endurance ability also have the biggest heart volumes. The 'sportsman's heart' is one which is accustomed to effort, and which is superior to the normal heart in many respects. The musculature of the sportsman's heart is made more powerful by the harmonious growth of all its compartments. With the increase in length and thickness of the muscle fibres comes increased capacity. The mitochondria of the heart-muscle fibres are also larger. A greater volume comes from the size increase of the heart chambers. The normal male heart has a capacity of 750 to 800ml. Sportsmen's hearts show a volume of 900 to 1200ml, and sometimes as much as 1700ml. Female hearts are normally of 400 to 550ml capacity, but with sport training can contain around 1000ml. The trained heart just works more economically than the untrained one.

Even the governing mechanisms of the human body, the hormone system and the involuntary nervous system, adapt themselves to the physical call for stamina. It is quite surprising how with endurance athletes the network of nerve endings is enlarged. The athlete's well-being and equilibrium at rest transfers itself to the parasympathetic nervous system, allowing better recovery, and the lowering of the heart rate. Highly-trained sportsmen have a resting pulse of 40 to 50 beats per minute. This shows that the heart, its circulation and all physical processes have been improved.

Basic principles of cycle training

Training concepts

In order to define the concept of training, we must first define words such as 'practice', 'fitness' and 'sport'.

By **practice** we understand the systematic repetition of desired movements or actions, with the aim of improving performance without any bodily changes in the organism. Practice is limited to the improvement of the ability to move and function.

By **fitness** we understand a situation of being in a good state of readiness, both physical and mental, to perform a given exercise. Even passive situations, like the ability to withstand heat or cold, come under the heading of fitness.

By **sport** we understand — in this context — a muscular commitment which is either competitive in character, or has the aim of achieving certain personal goals.

Training therefore has as its goal the preparation of sportsmen to reach high, even the highest levels of sporting performance. Each training session is a planned preparation process. In high-effort sports, training demands a personal commitment on both physical and psychological planes. Training makes the body anatomically and functionally suited to the desired purpose.

The training process

A training programme has to be meticulously planned. It is a highly responsible position, if you have to lead young sportsmen from youth or school levels up to the highest adult standards. With the current demands of top-level sport — sports such as swimming or gymnastics notably excepted — the training process can last some 12 to 15 years.
In the beginning comes the selection of the right young athletes. But you can only really decide if a young person is right for cycle sport once you have actually seen them perform. There is no other method of talent-scouting. The best way of finding the right young cyclists is

to give them as many possibilities to compete as possible.
Once the young talent has been found, it is up to the trainer to develop it, gradually, systematically and sympathetically, towards improvement and specialization. At the beginning the main consideration should be general athletic fitness, to condition the body's organs and systems to the maximum. Only much later does specialization become part of the training process, with the idea of developing a solid resistance to the stresses of competition. Riders who have only just finished their conditioning training cannot be expected to take as much as those who have performed for years under the demands of top competition. You can train beginners from 10 to 12 years old. Next step up the training ladder is the 14 to 18 age group. High-intensity training can begin only around 17 years, but cyclists are only really capable of sustained high performances from 25 or so, this ability lasting until 35 or 40, providing that training and life-style continue as they should. Cycle sport, especially road racing, belongs to the group of

sports which can be taken up at any age, providing that you don't insist on reaching the very top levels. You can even take it up at 35, and still show improvement through training, especially in stamina, for years afterwards.

The basics of lifting your performance levels

'Increasing the level of cycling performance' is a way in which you can develop and express yourself. Without exercise or physical demands on them, the functions of the human body waste away. It follows that, through exercise and physical demands, the body can adapt itself to assume greater and greater burdens — provided this exercise fulfils certain conditions. The concepts of imposed physical load, adaptation and increased performance are linked by physical laws.

1. In order to be able to help the adaptation of the body to greater imposed loads, training sessions must reach an optimal intensity and be of at least a given duration. Only

101

training sessions which upset the psycho-physical equilibrium to such an extent that they are considered a burden, can trigger off the adaptation processes. The intensity and extent of the training session should take account of the individual and his state of fitness. Too great or too little a load in training can have a detrimental effect.

2. Effort and recovery periods should change at a regular rate. Every worthwhile training session produces tiredness, and a transient lowering in physical capacity. But in the recovery period the desired functional and anatomical adaptation processes take place. In this way the organism regenerates itself, recovering to a level higher than before — a phenomenon known as overcompensation, the body building itself up to be able to meet such an effort again. This feature of overcompensation is the basis behind the idea of progressive overload in training. Effort, tiredness, recovery and overcompensation must be regarded as a single entity of the training process.

3. Behind every optimal effort is a training effect. But sometimes one can observe an apparent standstill in performance, although the efforts have been applied regularly and with sufficient intensity. Then suddenly at a given point there is a considerable performance improvement. This 'belated transformation' can be brought about by specially intensive training efforts, or by competition.

4. The higher the level of effort tolerance becomes, so must the effort demanded become greater too. For this reason the training effects are greater when fitness is at a low level. As performance levels get higher, the effect of repeated training sessions of similar intensity becomes less.

5. Training-related adaptation is reduced if the demands of the training programme are too low, or are not applied at the right time. The body always reacts to the demands which circumstances place upon it. With increasing fitness, the ability to recover also increases. Thus efforts can be made at shorter and shorter intervals. Therefore progressive overload only works when the increased effort is demanded during the overcompensation phase following the previous effort.

6. Stamina results especially from efforts of long duration but of low or medium intensity. Power and speed come from maximum or near-maximum efforts over short duration. The organism always reacts to the type of demands placed upon it.

Summarizing the six points, the planning of a training session should take account of the following factors:

☐ Effort intensity
☐ Proximity of effort
☐ Volume of effort
☐ Duration of effort
☐ Structure of effort
☐ Degree of effort
☐ Frequency of effort

Effort intensity
In cycling this is relative to the pedalling rate, the amount of power put into pedalling, and to the speed reached. To measure this you need to establish the moment of maximum output

during the training session or race. In order to stimulate the adaptation process in the cardio-vascular system, the intensity of effort must be such that the heart rate reaches at least 140 beats per minute. But the intensity should never be so high that the pedalling itself is affected.

Proximity of effort

This is a matter of time between different efforts during a training session. The better a rider's condition and his tolerance to effort, the more frequently the efforts can take place, and the longer they can last. The length of the gap between efforts depends on the speed of recovery. This is particularly important in interval training, repetition training and circuit training.

Volume of effort

This can be measured either by the distance covered during training, or by the duration of the effort periods. Efforts of a given intensity only have the best training effects when they are part of a training session which has the right volume. This can be judged if the efforts produce signs of fatigue. The fatigue should be such that its effects are felt for some time after the training finishes.

Duration of effort

This is the length of the effort, which will vary, depending on what kind of speciality the rider is being trained for.

For stamina training the efforts should last long enough for signs of fatigue to be clearly evident. Long series of efforts should produce fatigue and trigger off the recovery processes. At the end of the effort a drop in performance level should be noticed.

For power and speed training fatigue should not enter into the picture. Instead, the effort should be at a high pedalling rate against maximum resistance with maximum concentration on the task.

In order to improve stamina, the fatigue processes must be induced. The duration of effort should be at least half an hour to one hour. If the interval system is being used, then the effort periods should be between 8 and 12 minutes.

Structure of effort

By this we understand the quality of the training or the training session, essentially the relationship between the intensity and the volume of the effort. This structure changes according to the aim of the training session (strength, stamina, speed, technique, tactics). It also changes with the state of fitness. Splitting a training plan into various sections can only work if each section is properly structured. Then the goal of the whole process is achieved.

Degree of effort

A given effort can actually *feel* different, depending on the state of the rider at the time (how you feel). You can estimate the degree of effort by the degree of fatigue and the speed of recovery it produces. You can normally assume that a given effort is having good training results when it produces extreme fatigue. With this in mind you can choose between small, medium and large efforts.

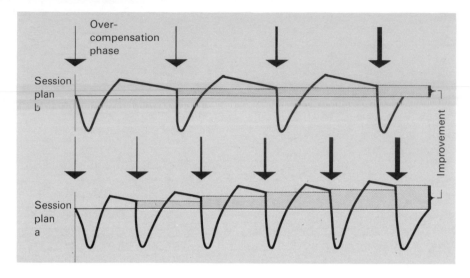

Over-compensation phase

Session plan b

Session plan a

Improvement

Training must follow on regularly and with sufficient frequency.
Above: low frequency, low improvement.
Below: greater frequency, greater improvement.

Frequency of effort

This depends on the structure of the effort, its degree, and the effort tolerance of the rider. Since the body recovers more quickly with increasing fitness the frequency of effort should also increase. A new effort should thus be made once the recovery from the previous one is completed. The new effort will have no worthwhile effect if the body has not recovered. The frequency and the structure of the efforts demanded should be in harmony. Normal frequency for a beginner would be 3 to 5 sessions per week, for the advanced rider 6 to 8 and for the top-class rider 8 to 12 sessions per week.

The path to top performance

In top-level training the rider should reach his own highest output level and either hold it as long as possible or improve it. This can only be achieved through years of basic, properly conceived, conditioning training. In high-level training the volume of effort is increased and so is its intensity. Thus the potential of the rider is increased. At the same time more specialized training is introduced, with the rider's speciality in mind. Technique and tactical skills are developed to the full.
Top-level performance increases relative to the increase in demands placed upon the body. It

is typically reached when the frequency of competition is high. High-intensity work in competition and training demands the maximum input by the rider. For this reason the development of personal qualities such as will-power, toughness, commitment and inspiration, is of paramount importance. These qualities determine whether the rider is ready to produce top performance over a long period. For this reason, in the training plan the structure of the effort — that is, the relationship between its volume and intensity — and the right balance between effort and recovery, are of utmost importance. Without a methodical training plan no sportsman can reach a peak. You must analyse the various factors in relation to the required level of performance in competition, and strive to adapt to that level through systematic training. But once you find that you can fulfil the various performance criteria, don't go wasting energy or introducing factors into your life which will lower performance level. The basis for reaching the levels you strive for, lies in the principles of adopting a *sportsman's life-style*:

Effort profile of various cycling events relative to their components of strength, speed and stamina.

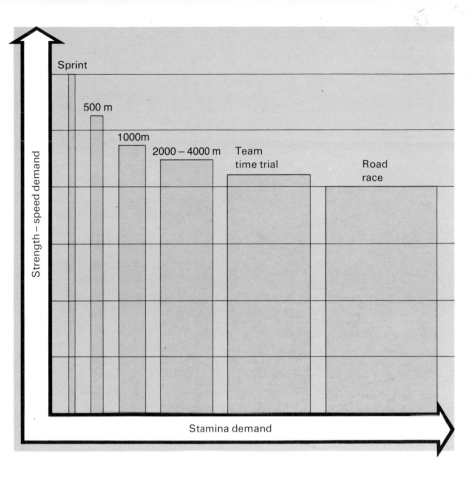

- ☐ Enriching sleep
- ☐ Regular daily programme
- ☐ Ideal nutrition
- ☐ Avoidance of indulgences (alcohol, nicotine, caffeine)
- ☐ Normal non-excessive sex life
- ☐ Regular care of your body
- ☐ Sensible, relaxing use of leisure time
- ☐ Orderly living conditions in quiet surroundings and in clean air.

The effect of training efforts is greater the more closely you can adhere to these principles. This way of life is essential for good health and fitness, and only by following it can a sportsman reach full potential.
High-performance training doesn't mean training without thinking; it also assumes that the whole sporting personality will develop to maturity along with the physical state.

A racing cyclist's performance profile

For the cyclist who rides for health and recreation it should be enough to be able to develop some stamina through the right kind of training. But we will consider the demands of cycle sport from the standpoint of the top rider and in this way even the spare-time cyclist can get an idea of what planned training is all about.
The required performance elements in cycle sport are:
1. Personal qualities (character, will-power, motivation, intellectual ability).
2. Conditional skills (stamina, speed, strength, suppleness).
3. Technique.
4. Tactics.
Each type of cycle race has its own set of requirements, especially in the department of conditional skills: stamina, speed and strength. Let us now take a look at the demands of the various kinds of cycle sport.

Road racing

Individual events

We can distinguish the following different kinds of individual road events for amateurs:

- ☐ Road races (120 to 180km or more).
- ☐ Circuit races and criteriums (60 to 100km).
- ☐ Time trials (up to 60km or more).
- ☐ Hill climbs (from 5 to 20km, usually ridden as time trials).

Road races are conducted from a massed start. For these you need a high degree of stamina with a high maximal oxygen uptake, using the body's adaptation mechanisms induced by training to the utmost. In addition the road rider needs high speed and sustained power, in order to react to the changing conditions of road racing. During breakaway attempts, prime sprints, uphill efforts and finishing sprints anaerobic capabilities are called upon in order to supply the required energy. A highly-trained road rider will, however, be able to meet some of these challenges through aerobic effort. A characteristic of a good rider is the ability to draw on fats as the source of energy for a greater part of the requirements of riding at high speed.

In **criteriums** the overall victory is often decided on points for intermediate sprints. Criteriums are run on short circuits, usually less than 2.5km. They call for accelerations out of every corner, and for every sprint. As well as a high degree of stamina, these events require a high anaerobic capacity, the ability to go deep into oxygen debt and still perform. A typical gear for criteriums is 52 x 16, so as well as acceleration power a high pedalling speed is necessary.

For **circuit races** similar qualities are necessary. These events are run on larger circuits.

Individual time trials also require a high degree of stamina. But in comparison to massed-start road races a higher strength element is needed, in order to be able to handle the necessary big gears. In the closing phases of a time trial there is some anaerobic work.

Hill climbs really belong to the time-trial section, but sometimes they are run as massed-start events. A high degree of stamina is necessary, along with a considerable amount of strength. Because some of the climb will be in the 'honking' style you need good all-round condition, especially strong arms and shoulder-girdle. Medium-height (160–170cm) and lightweight (55–65kg) riders have an advantage.

100km team time trials

Normally four men make up a team in these events, with the time of the third rider counting. The 100km team time trial demands constant high speed from all riders, driving themselves to the limit of their ability. This is not the normal 'slipstreaming' method of riding, whereby the rider in the shelter of the one in front can relax as long as he wants. In fact, the next turn at the front comes when he has only just recovered from his last effort. If one of the team has a bad period, then it reflects on the team time. So it is best if the four riders are matched in their capabilities and their riding style. When you think that nowadays the 100km distance is covered in about two hours, meaning an average of around 50kph, then you realize what kind of fitness each team member needs. The event demands a very high aerobic endurance, and the ability to pedal big gears (54 x 13 to 56 x 13). It also demands the use of a great deal of strength.

Stage races

There are stage races for amateurs and professionals. This event is virtually a series of races ridden one after the other, day after day — road races, time trials and hill climbs. It puts demands on the rider not equalled in any other sport. The distance to be covered is normally between 1000 and 4000km. Between each stage there are often only a few hours for recovery. Characteristically, a good stage-race rider has very highly developed stamina and a high maximal oxygen uptake. He also has the ability to burn fat for energy, and this can be seen by the measurable decrease of subcutaneous fat during a stage race. Despite this, the body-weight alters little, since the fat-free body-mass — the muscles — have increased somewhat. In order to keep his body-weight up, the stage-race rider must be able to take in large amounts of nourishment (around 6000-8000 calories). Apart from

Time trials: the race against the clock begins.

excellent stamina, such a rider will have, according to the state of the race, a need for high speed and strength. Since these qualities are not shared out equally among all riders, we find the emergence of various specialists — climbers, sprinters, time triallists, flat-road racers. But the eventual victory can only go to an all-round rider who has good support from his team. The most famous stage race, the Tour de France, has been run since 1903, and puts the human body to the toughest possible sporting test.

Cyclo-cross

These are races of around 28km over open country which has natural and man-made obstacles. At least two-thirds of the course should be rideable. Cyclo-cross events run from late autumn to the end of the winter, which has to be taken into account when a training plan is formulated. A good cyclo-cross rider has qualities similar to those of a good roadman. But because there is bound to be a certain amount of running with the bike on his shoulder the cyclo-cross rider needs to have the same athletic and gymnastic qualities as a cross-country runner. Results in cyclo-cross depend to a great degree on the type of course. On bad courses where there is a lot of running, the good runners are favoured. On courses which have plenty of fast riding sections, the gifted road riders will do better. Apart from conditional skills such as stamina, strength and speed, cyclo-cross riders need to be nimble, supple, skilful and have a perfect technique. Cyclo-cross races are good for winter training.

Cyclo-cross: Klaus-Peter Thaler, several times world champion.

Track events

There are a large number of track events, and one can differentiate here again between individual and team events (world championship events underlined):

Individual events

- ☐ Sprint
- ☐ Pursuit
- ☐ Time trial
- ☐ Handicap
- ☐ Points race
- ☐ Devil take the hindmost
- ☐ Tandem sprint
- ☐ Madison
- ☐ Motor-paced (stayer)
- ☐ Keirin

Team events

- ☐ Team pursuit
- ☐ Italian pursuit

Omnium events

- ☐ Consisting of individual and team events

The **sprint** takes place over two or three laps, with between two and four riders starting together, the time being taken over the final 200m. A sprint tournament will have heats, *repêchages* and more rounds leading to a final. The last 200m time is not all-important. What are needed are top sprinter qualities, high speed and quick reactions. Also needed are strength and power, and the ability to maintain maximum effort over a short period. A sprinter's muscles are

109

Dieter Berkmann: concentrating on a standstill tactic.

The **individual pursuit** is over a given distance (4000m for amateurs, 5000m for professionals, 3000m for women and juniors) or until one rider catches the other. Stamina is of paramount importance. But alongside this high aerobic capacity a good anaerobic quality is also important. Good road riders can put their aerobic qualities to advantage in individual pursuiting. Speed and strength also have a role to play, but not as much as in the sprint events.

Finish of a track sprint: Japan's Nakano just beats Dieter Berkmann.

Usually over 1000m, with standing or flying start, the **time-trial** demands a high anaerobic capacity, with the use of strength and speed. As with the sprinter, some degree of stamina, over short to middle distance, is useful.

Good stamina is essential for quick regeneration of the energy-rich phosphates (ATP and creatin), and for the rapid breakdown of any lactic acid which results from anaerobic effort.

In the **handicap race** the riders compete over a given distance, starting in reverse order of their ability. The strongest rider starts at the starting-line, while his opponents are given starts depending on their ability, spaced out at intervals of 5 to 10m.

From 1984 the **points race** will become an Olympic event. It is an individual event with a massed start, and a distance of up to 50km. During the race there are intermediate sprints, usually every ten laps. The first four places in each sprint get 5, 3, 2 and 1 points respectively, with double points for the final sprint.

predominantly of white, fast-twitch fibres. Sprinters are muscular types with powerful upper bodies. They must have a high anaerobic capacity. Their energy comes from the energy-rich phosphates and from glycogen.

Anyone gaining a lap on the rest of the field automatically takes precedence, no matter what the points totals are.

Devil take the Hindmost is a massed-start track race. At the end of each lap the last rider across the line is eliminated. The event distance depends on the size of the field.

In **tandem sprinting** two riders are mounted on one machine, and race over a distance of about 1500m. This demands high speed and strength, but good middle-range stamina is also helpful. A certain aerobic capacity and a high anaerobic capacity are necessary. The race speed is so high that the use of fat as energy is ruled out, so this comes instead from carbohydrate reserves.

Madison is an event in which two men race as a team over a given time or distance, the maximum for amateurs being 100km or three hours. It is a continuous relay race, the pairs being able to relay each other at will, as long as one rider from each team is racing at any given moment.

1000m time trial: Freddy Schmidtke, twice world junior champion.

Tandem.

111

swings off with two laps to go.

In **four-man team pursuits** two teams start simultaneously on opposite sides of the track. The winning team is the one which either catches the other, or completes the distance in the best time. The team time is taken when the front wheel of the third rider crosses the finish line, which means that teams try to finish virtually in line abreast. The team members must be in harmony, in the same way as in the road team time-trial event. Even at the high speeds of the track, top teams reduce the distance between the rear wheel of one rider and the front wheel of the next one to a few millimetres. Technique is everything, changes of the front rider needing to be exactly timed. The event needs high concentration, co-ordination, medium-range stamina, strength and speed. A fast pedalling rate on a fixed gear is essential.

Italian pursuit
Two teams of 6 to 8 riders start as in the team pursuit. At the end of each lap the leading rider swings off and retires, the result resting on when the final rider of each team crosses the line.

Motor-paced or stayer races are ridden on the track behind pacing motor-cycles, which means that speeds of 60kph are achieved over a distance of 100km. For the rider it is a question of maintaining the right distance behind the pacer, neither coming too close to the roller nor too far behind it. At a speed of 60–70kph in an indoor stadium a rider will experience a force of eight times his own weight on the bends. This means that the bicycle must be strengthened at various parts. Essential for success is long-distance stamina, married to speed and strength. The importance of concentration in this kind of race is such that the rider must never become badly fatigued, and for this reason a high degree of aerobic fitness is necessary.

The **Keirin** race began in Japan, and since 1980 has been a world championship event for professionals. Usually 6 or 8 riders start together, and are gradually built up to a finishing sprint by a pacemaker, who

Omnium
A collection of track races can count towards an omnium result. Points are given for each event, and added together for the final result.

Stayer racing: Wilfried Peffgen paced by Durst.

Keirin racing.

Indoor cycling
This can be split into acrobatic cycling, cycle-ball and cyclo-polo. In acrobatic cycling a high degree of physical control and technical skill is essential, as well as a certain degree of strength. For cycle-ball, a kind of game like football, speed, strength, skill and stamina are all desirable.

Above: six-day racing, and a conventional handover from Patrick Sercu to Dietrich Thurau.
Below: the same pair give a handsling change.

Summary
Although one can trace a different kind of profile for cyclists in the various disciplines, it is clear that basic stamina is important for a good performance, be it in track sprinting or indoor cycling. Varying degrees of strength and speed are also needed.

When it comes to a training plan, we need to distinguish between two aspects:

☐ Basic athlete's training
☐ Special training

Basic condition training

The basis of a special training plan for a racing cyclist is the building-up of general athletic condition. The aim of this build-up is to improve tangibly all the muscle groups and bodily systems, so that they will be better able to tolerate specialized training. This basic athletic development is particularly important for young riders. The longer you train, the more this concern for basic condition can fade into the background as more specialized training takes its place. As part of the daily routine, you should become accustomed to doing exercises for 5 or 10 minutes first thing in the morning. This useful habit makes for a healthy life-style, and brings the body from its resting state into readiness for activity.

There are all sorts of sporting activities which can be used to promote general condition. They are sports which use many types of muscle groups and body systems, either in turn or simultaneously. For example:

- [ ] Cross-country skiing
- [ ] Cross-country running
- [ ] Cyclo-cross
- [ ] Gymnastics
- [ ] Weight training
- [ ] Swimming
- [ ] Team games
- [ ] Speed skating
- [ ] Ice hockey

Ideal for a cyclist is **circuit training,** which is a selection or 'circuit' of several exercises, some using apparatus, others not.

The lengths of the activities and the rests in between them should be set to provide a kind of interval training, so that stamina is built up. You can complete several circuits in an hour's work-out. This form of training is so important that I shall give two suggested circuits, illustrated on the following pages:

Circuit 1
(apparatus: bench, wall-bars, beam)

1. Prone position, lifting arms and legs
2. Press-ups
3. Single-knee bending, alternate legs
4. Pull-ups
5. Standing jumps over a bench
6. Sit-ups on an inclined bench

Circuit 2
(apparatus: bench, wall-bars, dumb-bells)

1. Sideways lifting on inclined bench
2. Jumping from a crouch position
3. Supine lying, lifting legs and arms
4./5. Hopping over a bench
6. Leg lifts on inclined bench

As a racing cyclist you should always keep active, have some way of staying in shape. If you can't get out on the bike, then it is better to do 10 to 20 minutes of exercises than do nothing at all. For cyclists it is specially important to exercise muscle groups that are used to only a small extent in cycling, such as the upper body, arm muscles, shoulder-girdle and spine. A good cyclist should start the day with effective **morning exercises,** the aim being to stretch the muscles, ligaments and tendons through regular exercise, and to strengthen weak muscles. The real exercises should be preceded by a few looseners, to allow you to perform the exercises better. You can either work from top to toe or vice versa; for example, head-rolling, arm-circling, pelvis circling, sideways, back and forward bending, leg lifting and circling, foot circling. The 'real' exercises should be aimed at strengthening the muscles and should be followed by some breathing exercises.

Circuit 1
(apparatus: bench, wall-bars, beam)
1. Prone position, lifting arms and legs.
2. Press-ups.
3. Single-knee bending, alternate legs.
4. Pull-ups.
5. Standing jumps over a bench.
6. Sit-ups on inclined bench.

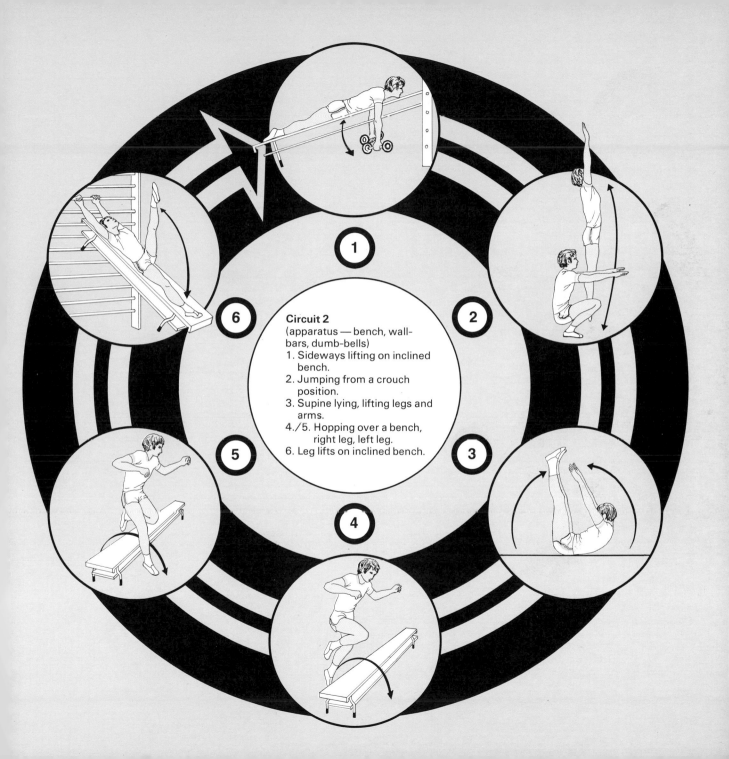

Circuit 2
(apparatus — bench, wall-bars, dumb-bells)
1. Sideways lifting on inclined bench.
2. Jumping from a crouch position.
3. Supine lying, lifting legs and arms.
4./5. Hopping over a bench, right leg, left leg.
6. Leg lifts on inclined bench.

Morning exercises First, easy head rolling in both directions (1: 10 times) then shoulder shrugging (2) forwards and backwards (10 times). Arm-circling (3) backwards and forwards (20 times), then forward and backward bending (4: 10 times). Sideways bending to right and left (6: 10 times). Alternate toe touching with feet astride (5), right hand to left toe and vice versa (15 times), then staying in the same position, twist the body and reach backwards to touch left heel with right hand, then right heel with left hand (7) in turn (5 times). Feet even further apart, fold your arms and bend forward (8) keeping back straight and head up, trying to touch the floor with the elbows and easing back again. Lift your body, then down again (9) to grasp the ankles, then pulling down with the back straight to stretch the lumbar region. Up again, then shift the body weight over alternate feet (10). Finally foot circling (11: 10 times) and press-ups (12: 20 to 50 times).

4

5

6

7

10

11

12

Relaxation (3 minutes)

Yoga exercise sequence

The best and most proven system for stretching muscles and for making the spine supple is yoga. During a yoga exercise session the spine is flexed, extended and at the end of the exercises twisted and turned. In this way the blood circulation to the spine, and its flexibility, are markedly improved. The necessary concentration and breathing control for the exercises can be turned to advantage by the racing cyclist. If you wish to progress further with yoga, you can consult books or go to classes. Just to begin with, here is a series of recommended exercises. The essence of yoga is not in a series of increasingly complex physical contortions, but in the performance of exercises which bring your whole body into consciousness, and make you in turn aware of your body. Modern high-performance training has a similar goal, but achieves it differently. For this reason simple yoga exercises are an ideal complement to high-performance training.

The Tongs (2 minutes)

Shoulder stand (1 minute)

The Cobra (1 minute)

The Twist (1 minute each direction)

The Plough (2 minutes)

The Fish (1 minute)

The Bow (1 minute)

The Locust (1 minute)

Breathing (3 minutes)

Headstand (1 to 10 minutes)

Relaxation (3 minutes)

Speciality training

For speciality training you need special methods. You need to build up the muscle groups and body systems which are particularly stressed in the type of cycle racing you have chosen. But the form of training cannot be such that it concentrates only on one aspect. It should ideally work to improve all the required qualities. It is not good only training for stamina, although good stamina is a basis for all types of cycle racing. Instead, your training should have the goal of building up speed, strength, suppleness, technique and tactics at the same time. Each type of cycle racing has a need for these qualities, but the relative proportion of each varies according to the type. The important part is not **how many** kilometres you cover, but **the way in which** those kilometres are covered. The efforts you produce in training should be chosen and measured so that they have the express aim of improving a particular kind of performance. In seeking the right kind of training effect, the following factors come into play.

☐ Duration of training
☐ Intensity of effort (speed)
☐ Size of gear (power input, pedalling rate)
☐ The time lapse between efforts

These factors vary according to the aim of the training session.

Stamina training

The development of stamina allows a rider to tackle an event with full commitment, a relaxed style, the correct technique and tactics. The necessary speed should be reached by an ideal combination of pedalling power and pedalling rate, and then maintained. As well as the basic stamina, the rider should have a stamina type which is specific to the sort of competition envisaged. This is relative to the duration of the effort during the competition. Thus stamina can be split into several types:

☐ Long-term stamina
☐ Middle-term stamina
☐ Short-term stamina
☐ Strength stamina
☐ Speed stamina

Long-term stamina

This is necessary for sporting performances which last from 10 minutes to several hours. Road racing belongs to this category. The effort is predominantly aerobic. Long-term efforts benefit all the systems of the body. The more oxygen the body can take up during a given unit of time, the greater is its stamina. Maximal oxygen uptake is also called aerobic capacity. Anaerobic processes come into action during road racing only in specific conditions, such as breakaway attempts, sprints, and hill climbs.

Middle-term stamina

This kind of quality is needed for events which last between 2 and 10 minutes. It is needed for track events such as tandem sprinting, individual and team pursuiting. It demands high aerobic and anaerobic capacities. Good strength stamina, and speed

stamina also help performances in this kind of event.

Short-term stamina
This form of stamina is needed for a distance which takes between 45 seconds and 2 minutes to cover, such as track sprints and kilometre time trials. It is predominantly anaerobic. In addition, good performances in such events demand strength and speed stamina. A track sprint is 70 to 80 per cent anaerobic, but good aerobic capacity is also necessary here. The rider must build up the ability to tolerate a high degree of lactic acid in his muscles, which is best promoted during repetition and interval training.

Strength stamina
This idea represents an ability to display strength at the same time as stamina. The shorter the race distance, the more strength stamina is necessary. Even in longer events, such as road races, a certain degree of strength stamina can be helpful.

Speed stamina
This means the ability to withstand fatigue during efforts which are predominantly anaerobic and are carried out at sub-maximal or maximal speed. In cycling terms, this is the ability to push big gears faster (sprints, breakaway attempts, track events). The essentials for speed stamina are a faultless riding style and good basic stamina.

Methods of stamina training
Through stamina training, both basic stamina and competition-specific stamina can be developed. A high degree of basic stamina is essential for all branches of cycle sport. The greater part of training must be centred on developing the aerobic capacity, the ability to take up and use oxygen. There are four types of training for developing stamina:

1. Long-distance training
   - ☐ Continuous method
   - ☐ Changing method
   - ☐ Fartlek
2. Interval method
   - ☐ Long intervals
   - ☐ Medium intervals
   - ☐ Short intervals
3. Repetition method
4. Competition and control methods

Long-distance training method
This lays the foundations for the build-up of basic stamina. It heightens the general tolerance to effort and improves the body's recovery systems. It is the main training method, particularly in the period of preparation. Long-distance training consists of longer efforts which are not interspersed with rests. The speed can be constant or changing. Apart from serving the cardio-vascular circulation, it also specially improves the energy-producing metabolic processes and makes them more economic. The duration of the effort should be not less than 30 minutes, and preferably an hour or two. Top riders have such training sessions lasting 5, 6 or more hours. The average speed should reach around 30kph, and medium gears should be ridden. Using the **continuous method,** the speed is maintained over a long period, the heart's pulse rate reaching 150 to 170 beats per minute with the experienced rider. Untrained riders or those who have trained only a little should reckon the desirable pulse rate by this formula: 180 minus your age. This means that a 40-year-old should train at

around 140 beats per minute. As fitness improves, so can the heart rate at which you train increase. Using the **changing or repetition method,** which is also good for strength and speed training, predetermined distances (say 100 to 200m) are covered at such a high speed that lactic acid is produced in the muscles. The pauses in between efforts should be long enough to allow the lactic acid to be dispersed.

Fartlek (literally: 'go as you please') is a game with speed. This game can revolve around the terrain, for instance you can increase effort on hills, or when town signs come up, going back to an easier pace afterwards. You make your own rules.

Interval methods

Interval training consists of carefully planned effort and recovery periods. The pauses between efforts are however not quite long enough to allow the body to recover completely. The new effort should be commenced when the heart-beat has dropped to 120–130, in other words before the recovery process is complete. In the **short interval method,** the effort phase lasts between about 15 seconds and 2 minutes.

In the **medium interval method,** it lasts 2 to 8 minutes.

In the **long interval method,** it lasts 8 to 15 minutes.

The shorter the period of effort, the more intensive it must be. The long interval method is used to build up basic stamina. The short interval method above all develops speed stamina. Through the correct application of the different interval methods you can develop the kind of stamina necessary for your type of competition. For example, the road rider should choose a long interval ridden at 40kph.

If you choose an interval with high speed, it is referred to as an **intensive interval effort;** when the speed is lower and the effort longer, it is **an extensive interval effort.**

Repetition effort

In repetition training you reproduce and repeat the effort required in competition, at intervals which allow the body to recover completely.

Gear, pedalling rate and speed should be exactly those which can be expected in a race. You can even put in simulated prime sprints or breakaway efforts. The difference between this and interval training lies in the duration of the pauses between efforts. With interval training the new effort begins before recovery is complete, whereas in repetition training the recovery must be complete before the new effort begins.

Competition and control methods

In the course of a training plan, and at set times, it is necessary to check the progress of your performances, and thus to set new training goals.

Competition and control methods revolve around the race circuit itself. Road riders use these methods to work out how long they need to cover a known circuit or course in time trial. Track riders do a similar exercise but over their track distances. Each method has its effects, not only on the body processes, the circulation and the nervous system, but also on the psychological condition of the rider. The training plan should not employ just one method, but instead should ring the changes, using several of the methods most appropriate to the rider's needs. Monotony in training is counter-productive. Which stamina training method you choose to concentrate upon depends on the type of racing you are aiming at — for example, short interval training is most helpful for track events. Using the different stamina training methods will also improve the rider's psychological tolerance to effort. Continuous stamina training improves the will-power which the road rider needs so much, while short and medium interval training develops the explosive determination prized by the sprinter and other track riders.

Also, by varying the gear, speed stamina and strength stamina can be improved.

Strength training

Here we must distinguish between maximum strength (or static maximum strength), power (or dynamic strength) and strength stamina.

By **maximum strength** we understand the strength which the sportsman can develop through maximum muscle effort. By **power**, we understand a sportsman's ability to overcome high resistance at a high speed. By **strength stamina** we understand the sportsman's resistance to fatigue in long-lasting efforts.

A high degree of strength stamina is useful for the road rider, while good power and maximum strength are necessary for track. When he makes his effort from zero, a track sprinter puts some 350 to 380kg behind his pedal thrusts. Good power is important for prime sprints and finishing sprints which the road rider must face. A road rider should increase his strength without increasing muscle bulk greatly, which can be done by using low and medium resistance and overcoming them quickly. In other words, using low to medium gears and pedalling them fast.

Strength training methods

Maximum strength is increased by using medium to high gears at 80 to 100 per cent effort. One should make 2 to 8 such efforts, in the form of sprints, which should last some 30 seconds each. A further series of sprints should follow after a break which allows the rider to recover completely, usually between 3 and 5 minutes. Because such training efforts demand a high degree of concentration, they should take place early in your training session and not at the end. As you become more and more tired, a medium or sub-maximal effort feels like a maximal effort; this means that the intensity of effort must fall after several series of efforts. Normally four or five sprint series are sufficient, within a training session, to develop maximum strength.

In **power training** the pedalling rate is increased, but the maximum strength is also increased. The more you concentrate on maximum strength, the lower will be your pedalling rate, while the more you concentrate on pedalling speed, the lower your maximum strength will be. The idea is to gain the

right balance between the two situations, depending on your preference (your chosen style of racing). If you want to train for speed, then you have to pedal low and medium gears as fast as possible (120–150rpm). The essence of fast pedalling ability is in building up your central nervous system for this quick, repetitive series of movements. For this you need concentration. But you should not do power training when you are tired. Once again you train in series of 4 to 5 regularly spaced speed efforts. Between each series you allow a complete recovery period of 3 to 5 minutes, to allow the body and the nervous system to recuperate. During each period of effort, you must concentrate on achieving that maximum pedalling rate. With power and maximum strength training, the load should not be such that the actual exercise starts to suffer. If your pedalling style begins to disintegrate, then the effort is too great, so either the load (gear) or the pedalling rate should be reduced.

The goal of **strength stamina training** is a very high volume of effort, in other words overcoming a high resistance. It means you should be covering your training route very quickly, using high gears. You can develop this ability by using high gears in training, but obviously you will be pedalling at a lower rate. The duration of this kind of training effort should be 30 to 50 minutes. However, if you choose to ride medium gears at high pedalling rates to bring the leg muscles to exhaustion point, then the effort time (training time minus pauses) need be only 10 to 15 minutes. Best for training strength stamina are the interval (medium and long intervals) and repetition training methods. Apart from the nominated training methods, race-specific stamina, speed and strength are specially improved by **competition** itself. This element of competition is a necessary factor for the improvement of your performance. Experience of races improves toughness, tolerance of effort, and the skills of technique and tactics.

Flexibility training

Good flexibility is also a necessity for top performance. Supple joints improve the economy of your efforts and your pedalling. Poor flexibility means that your joints will move in a reduced range and so be more liable to sprains, and that you will certainly use more energy. The rider who has a reserve of suppleness will be better equipped to handle the changing circumstances of a race than a rider with poor basic suppleness. For this reason I recommend riders indulge in some form of gym work, with loosening and relaxation exercises included. The flexibility of the various joints (spine, hips, knees and ankles) is much improved by stretching exercises. Such exercises should be to the limit of the current flexibility, so that progress is made. My earlier comments about morning exercises and yoga sessions are also very important in the special training of the racing cyclist. One part of gymnastics improves the strength of muscle groups which are little exercised by cycling. It is particularly important for the more mature athlete to be careful how he performs these flexibility exercises.

Perfection of technique

As the cyclist puts in more and more years of training, so his technique improves. The process of good pedalling, which road and track rider must relearn each year, becomes more instinctive as time goes on.

For road riders

The **road rider** will learn how to take corners correctly, how to avoid obstacles, how to climb hills and mountains using the 'honking' style, how to take descents fast but safely. Slipstreaming and wheel-following can be improved, the riding style brought closer and closer to that of the great riders: parallel movement of the legs, a relaxed upper body, loose and easy movement all round.

In training sessions, especially for basic stamina using low and medium gears, a rider can always benefit from this extra 'schooling' in technique. If riders are equal in ability, then the one with the better technique will always come out ahead.

For cyclo-cross riders

Anyone aiming at **cyclo-cross** needs to train not only his basic condition, but also his technical skills and agility. You must practise slipping feet into toe-clips quickly and getting off the mark sharply.

For track riders

Because of the high centrifugal force on the bends, **track riders** must develop a very good technique here. Taking the wrong line on corners just loses time. Track sprinters have to practise their standstill technique, which demands great concentration and skill. Track riders must master many riding techniques, and in particular the track sprinter must have the ability to produce pedalling bursts of 140rpm. In team pursuiting the art of wheel-following and changing must be continually improved. In Madisons and six-day races the changing technique must be perfect, otherwise valuable strength is wasted. The kilometre time trial rider must cover the distance at maximum concentration and top speed. Riding directly on the track's datum line (the shortest line around the perimeter) must be practised so the rider covers no unnecessary extra distance. The motor-paced rider competes in the slipstream of his pacer at 70kph and more. Rider and pacer must develop unity, so that maximum speed is maintained with minimum effort.

Basics of tactics

On the track

In **track racing** technique and tactics run close together, and sometimes overlap. Psychological skills and determination are of the greatest importance, for your opponent must be mastered psychologically as well as physically.

Race experience counts for a lot. In track sprinting and kilometre time trials reaction time is important. In individual and tandem sprinting you have to watch your opponents. In individual and team pursuiting the principle is to go faster than your opponent, but tactics in this type of racing are to measure your effort so as to get maximum effort spread over the distance, no more and no less.

On the road

In **road racing,** because of the length of the course, the number of opponents and the constantly changing terrain, there are a great many more tactics to consider.

Tactical principles in road racing

As far as possible, before the race you should study the course map and profile, and choose your gearing accordingly. You should always gear as low as is practicable, so that good, easy pedalling style can be maintained.

Before the race you should warm up, lengthening the warm-up if the race distance is shorter. During the race, you should try to stay in the front third of the bunch. Only this way can you see how the race is developing, and be best placed to react to breakaway attempts. If, because of a sidewind, echelons have formed, you should always attempt to be in the front echelon, otherwise you will be in the wind too much and thus waste strength (see illustration). On flat roads in windy conditions you can tear the bunch apart, by putting them, as racing men say, into the gutter. A few riders with similar aims can, if the wind is coming from the right, form an echelon on the left of the road and go hard. The riders in the echelon can share the work, but the rest of the field are more or less in the wind with little or no

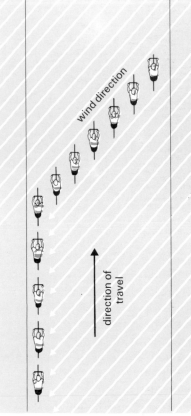

Echelons and 'putting someone in the gutter'.
The wind is from the right. The echelon spreads out to the left, leaving a tail of riders riding in the left-hand gutter, one behind the other, none getting sufficient shelter from the man in front.

'Throwing the bike' — the last effort in a finishing sprint.

shelter. As the only thing to do is to ride close behind the one in front, a long tail of riders forms. Some riders, unable to hang on to the one in front, will fall back, and gaps open. Usually new echelons form behind the leading one, which pulls gradually ahead.

If, as a result of this tactic, you find yourself in one of the chasing echelons, you have to do your utmost to get up to the front one — if you are strong enough. It means a maximum-speed effort for a few hundred metres, and joining the front echelon on the windy side. Once installed, you should immediately take your share of the pacing work in front.

There is no point in joining the echelon at the tail end of it, since all you will do is tire and fall back again. It is also no good trying to get your front wheel between the rear wheel of the next rider and the edge of the road. You will have nowhere to go except backwards.

A good rider is active in an event as long as his strength lasts, and doesn't just stay in the main bunch, hanging on to the back wheel of the rider in front. If you want to succeed, you must attack. You must have the courage to try to break away. But senseless breakaway attempts bring nothing except a waste of energy. The best moment to get away is when the other riders' instinct is to take a breather, or when no breakaway attempts are expected. The idea is to spurt clear of the field on the windward side, trying to put enough daylight behind you so that nobody else can get into your slipstream. For the first 1000m give it everything — and don't look back. When you do look round, it is to assess how successful the attempt has been. If you haven't got clear, then ease back into the front of the bunch, change down and take a

breather. Make the decision to look for the next opportunity, and the next — until you succeed! You should never attack from the head of the bunch. And it is better not to break away alone — that takes too much energy.

During a race you should eat regularly, but never just before a climb, when you are leading the field, or a group.

When you relinquish the lead after your turn in front, it should always be to the sheltered side. Just before swinging over, kick forward slightly and then ease back — but before doing so, make sure with a quick glance that the next man is where you expect him to be.

You must be prepared if it looks as though there is going to be a big-bunch finish. This means trying to be among the first 10 to 15 riders during the closing kilometres. Then, with a kilometre to go, watch for the right position for the sprint, one which will give you plenty of shelter but enough room to get out when you want to pass the rider or riders in front. Every sprint finish is different. Tactics vary according to the situation. And don't forget that your opponents will be throwing their bikes forward at the finish line (see illustration).

There are other basic tactics for road riders, but these are the most important.

Circuit races, cyclo-crosses and time trials have their own tactical aspects. The best way to learn them is to get as much racing experience as possible.

The training plan

The various exercises and purposes of training cannot be carried out in one training session. Training needs systematic planning, which brings in the right elements at the appropriate moment.

On principle the first aim of the rider during the course of his training should be to improve his basic stamina. At the same time he can work at perfecting his technique. Then, building on this basic condition, he can introduce training specific to his speciality and the type of stamina needed. But development doesn't happen at a regular rate. Instead it happens in phases, which can be distinguished in all training processes:

☐ Acquiring the necessary sporting ability

☐ Relative stabilization

☐ Temporary loss of sporting form

These stages or phases keep on repeating themselves throughout the training process, while sporting ability continues to improve.

Because of this, the body's regulating process, the training effort should not be constant. You must suit your training to this cyclical progression. We should here identify certain cycles within the training process, named according to how long they last:

1. Macrocycles: half-year cycles, yearly cycles (in the form of period cycles), cycles of several years

2. Mesocycles: cycles of three to six weeks

3. Microcycles: cycles of about a week

You can expect the best performance improvement if the training is regulated with the help of this cyclical idea, and the training effort is suited to it.

Macrocycles (period cycles)

A macrocycle generally embraces the training plan for a whole year. It is characterized by the periodic revision of goals, exercises and content of the individual training sessions. Such a periodic cycle would be split, over a year, into the following periods:

☐ Preparation period
☐ Competition period
☐ Transition period

The sportsman cannot maintain his optimum performance level throughout a whole year, but instead he produces that level of performance for certain major events or periods during the year. Depending on how many fitness peaks in a year the training process produces, it is referred to as a simple or multiple periodization of the training process. In high endurance sports such as road racing there is generally one long-term goal (such as a world championship) and this can be the object of simple periodization in training. In sports with short duration and high power requirements (such as track racing) a multiple periodization is required.

Cross-country running in winter.

Preparation period

This is divided into two stages with different points of concentration and aims. These are dictated, among other considerations, by the weather conditions.

The **first stage** of the preparation period for road sport embraces **winter training.** Training in this stage is characterized by low intensity (i.e. riding on low gears) and by how much the weather conditions will permit. In this stage, the build-up is in effort tolerance, pedalling technique and basic stamina. The first stage of the preparation period should take up at least one-third of the total period cycle — thus, in a simple periodization of the training year, some four months at least, corresponding to three mesocycles. In this time basic athletic training is of great importance. Because of the weather the cyclist will often have to leave his bike alone and maintain his work in some other way. Cross-country running, cross-country skiing, weight training, circuit training, swimming, games, are all possible. Some three or four training sessions per week should keep the athletic build-up

going. In winter training you should nevertheless try to do as much sport-related on-the-bike training as possible. Another way to do this is by using **ergometer training.** This can very easily be incorporated into a training programme, and by variation of the pedalling rate and the resistance (in watts) it can fulfil

Cross-country skiing.

various training needs. Training time on the ergometer should be between 30 and 60 minutes. There are a great number of ergometers (exercise cycles) on the market, and it is important to choose one on which your normal riding position can be simulated. Thus you can use it to improve pedalling as well as sport-specific

qualities such as strength, speed and stamina — short, medium and long-duration. In order to keep an eye on your pedalling, it is useful to set up a mirror. Some kind of fan or other ventilation will aid the evaporation of sweat and allows the body's temperature regulators to function properly. A tape recorder with music, language courses or similar diversions helps to keep away boredom. Because of the high amount of sweat loss with ergometer training (one to two litres per session) it is important to replace liquid and mineral losses. With this taken care of, three to four sessions a week on the ergometer are quite possible.

Ergometer training plans
With the bicycle ergometer you can train well, specially when conditions outside are bad. But it is important that the training programme should be progressive and right for the individual, and this is best done with the aid of your own pulse rate. The duration of the training sessions should be 30 to 60 minutes. In addition, you will need 5 minutes' warm-up and 10 minutes' winding-down afterwards.

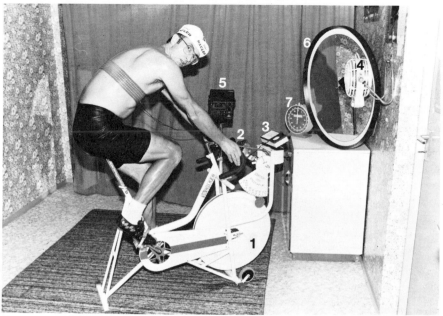

Ergometer training, using a Wilken-Monark ergometer.
1. Large driving wheel.   2. Pedal rev counter.   3. Pulse counter.   4. Fan.
5. Cassette recorder.   6. Mirror   7. Clock.

The focus of the training (stamina, speed, maximum strength, power etc) should change daily, which should take care of boredom and over-training.
When estimating your short effort for maximum strength (half a minute) you should refer to the test which establishes the highest level of effort you can maintain for 3 minutes. Over the half-minute you will of course be able to produce an even higher level of effort.

Strength training.

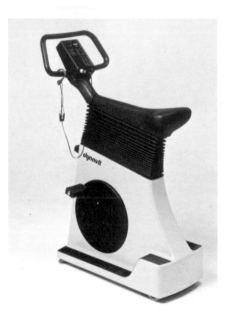

Training ergometer: Dynavit Meditronic.

With these training programmes it is important to keep a close watch on maintaining the given pedalling rate. You can change the resistance to suit your own fitness.
Normal settings for medical ergometer cycles used by cyclists are as follows: starting-point 150 watts (100 for women). Increase by 50 watts every 3 minutes until either exhaustion point is reached, or the target heart rate is achieved.

Training plan A

For riders whose maximum effort level lies around 200 watts.

Maximum strength/power   Monday

Watts	kp	Rpm	Min	Reps	
100	0.8	120	5		Warm-up
240	2.0	120	0.5	5 ×	← Set
80	0.8	100	1.5		
90	0.8	110	2		Rest
260	2.3	115	0.65	5 ×	← Set
80	0.8	100	1.5		
90	0.8	110	2		Rest
270	2.5	105	0.5	5 ×	← Set
80	0.8	100	1.5		
90	0.8	110	2		Rest
270	2.8	95	0.5	5 ×	← Set
80	0.8	100	1.5		
90	0.8	110	2		Rest
280	3.1	90	0.5	5 ×	← Set
80	0.8	100	1.5		
95	0.8	120	12		Warm-down

kp = kilopounds		Min = minutes	
Rpm = revs per minute		Reps = repetitions	

Stamina (strength oriented)   Tuesday

Watts	kp	Rpm	Min	Reps
90	0.8	120	5	
160	1.7	95	10	
80	0.8	100	2	5 ×
90	0.8	120	10	

Speed stamina   Wednesday

Watts	kp	Rpm	Min	Reps
95	0.8	110	5	
95	0.9	110	1	
100	0.9	115	1	
105	0.9	120	1	
110	0.9	125	1	
115	0.9	130	1	
115	0.9	130	1	7 ×
110	0.9	125	1	
105	0.9	120	1	
100	0.9	115	1	
95	0.9	110	1	
90	0.8	120	5	

Stamina (speed oriented)   Thursday/Saturday

Watts	kp	Rpm	Min	Reps
90	0.8	120	5	
150	1.4	105	5	
155	1.45	110	5	5 ×
80	0.8	100	2	
90	0.8	120	10	

Fartlek   Friday/Sunday

Watts	kp	Rpm	Min
90	0.8	120	5
125	1.2	110	5
105	0.9	120	5
160	1.5	110	5
125	1.2	110	5
160	1.7	95	5
90	0.8	120	5
160	1.7	95	5
90	0.8	120	5
100	0.9	115	5
160	1.7	95	5
90	0.8	120	5
125	1.2	110	5
105	0.9	120	5
90	0.8	120	5

Training on rollers allows you to keep warm and to practise your pedalling style. It is only possible to increase the effort slightly, since the pedalling resistance can hardly be varied. Sometimes

Training on the rollers.

during the course of a mesocycle (four to six weeks) you can test progress either on the open road or on an ergometer. Then the next mesocycle effort requirements should be suited to the progress made.

Training plan B

For riders whose maximum effort level lies around 350 watts.

Maximum strength/power		Monday			
Watts	kp	Rpm	Min	Reps	
120	1.0	120	5		Warm-up
420	3.5	120	0.5	5 ×	← Set
100	1.0	100	1.5		
110	1.0	110	2		Rest
460	4.0	115	0.5	5 ×	← Set
100	1.0	100	1.5		
110	1.0	110	2		Rest
470	4.5	105	0.5	5 ×	← Set
100	1.0	100	1.5		
110	1.0	110	2		Rest
475	5.0	95	0.5	5 ×	← Set
100	1.0	110	1.5		
110	1.0	110	2		Rest
495	5.5	90	0.5	5 ×	← Set
100	1.0	110	1.5		
120	1.0	120	12		Warm-down

138

Stamina (strength oriented)   Tuesday

Watts	kp	Rpm	Min	Reps
120	1.0	120	5	
285	3.0	95	10	5 ×
100	1.0	100	2	5 ×
120	1.0	120	10	

Stamina (speed oriented)   Thursday/Saturday

Watts	kp	Rpm	Min	Reps
120	1.0	120	5	
265	2.5	105	5	
275	2.5	110	5	5 ×
100	1.0	100	2	
120	1.0	120	10	

Speed stamina   Wednesday

Watts	kp	Rpm	Min	Reps
165	1.5	110	5	
165	1.5	110	1	
173	1.5	115	1	
180	1.5	120	1	
188	1.5	125	1	
195	1.5	130	1	
195	1.5	130	1	7 ×
188	1.5	125	1	
180	1.5	120	1	
173	1.5	115	1	
165	1.5	110	1	
120	1.0	120	5	

Fartlek   Friday/Sunday

Watts	kp	Rpm	Min
120	1.0	120	5
220	2.0	110	5
180	1.5	120	5
275	2.5	110	5
220	2.0	110	5
285	3.0	95	5
120	1.0	120	5
285	3.0	95	5
120	1.0	120	5
175	1.5	115	5
285	3.0	95	5
120	1.0	120	5
220	2.0	110	5
180	1.5	120	5
120	1.0	120	5

The **second stage** of the preparation period in cycling includes training during the **early part of the year**. It serves to make the fitness already achieved more specific to competition. Apart from improving basic stamina, it builds up the particular kind of stamina (long-term, medium or short-term) which is specific to the chosen form of racing. Training sessions of high volume but low intensity are varied with those of lower volume but greater intensity. Through long training runs at low intensity (low gears) you tend to mobilize your fat reserves for energy. This means that your weight reduces towards racing weight. Apart from basic and specific stamina, other training goals are strength and speed, in the proportions necessary for your chosen events.

In this preparation period cyclists usually put away between 3000 and 10,000km on small to medium gears. If it is possible, a training camp in better weather conditions (Spain, Majorca, South of France, Italy) will allow you to do the necessary increased volume of training in fairly stable weather. Don't underestimate the value of this change of scenery. The unfamiliar countryside, the warmer atmosphere, the sea air, all help to stop training becoming monotonous.

Through spending at least three weeks at altitude (over 2000m) the body can make great strides in fitness. You can reach top form more quickly if your preparation period has included altitude training.

Competition period

Through taking part in competition (cycle races) the competitive edge will be sharpened and stabilised, so that when the planned major events take place, you will be able to produce the best possible races. During the competition period the training volume (distance) will be maintained, in order to stabilise basic stamina. But since in this period there will be intensity through the races themselves, the intensity element in training can be reduced accordingly. In principle, a rider can race more and more frequently as he puts more years of training behind him. A rider who has been training for ten years is tough enough to cope with a hard event every week. Growing riders should husband their energies. Normally you can expect to reach top form some 6 to 10 weeks after the start of the competition period. After hard races it is recommended to change your training methods to help active recovery — that is, to ride long distances at low intensity, until the body has completely recuperated, mentally and physically. You can even include a complete rest day from time to time. During the competition period you can establish how many races are necessary to produce top form and hold it, and how much rest time between races is necessary.

Build-up of the competition period in cycles

Cycle	Configuration	Aims
1st cycle (about 4–8 weeks)	Gradual movement towards optimal racing frequency. Build-up races with increasing degrees of difficulty, one or two main events at the end of the cycle. Volume of effort in training somewhat reduced according to race frequency and effort tolerance.	Rapid improvement in racing performance. Attainment of qualifying standards. Build-up of race toughness. Recognition of strengths and weaknesses. Gathering of race experience and the testing of tactical foundations. The perfection of technique in race conditions.
2nd cycle (about 4 weeks)	Concentration on training; raising of the effort volume and training frequency; one race only; no restrictions on training.	Making good any weaknesses already established in competition.
3rd cycle (about 4 weeks)	Races with higher degree of difficulty than in the first cycle. Build-up races to qualifying events or trials. Gradual reduction of the effort volume in training, with regard to the demands of the type of racing chosen.	Stabilising race fitness. Preparation for qualifying races or trials. Testing yourself under the toughest of racing conditions.
4th cycle (about 4–5 weeks)	Special preparation for the main event of the year.	

Transition period

At the end of the competition period the rider needs a period of recuperation, both in physical strength and mental condition. The aim of the transition period is the recovery of the body's whole strength — leading into the preparation period for the next year. With a top-class rider, this transition period should not last too long, certainly no more than four weeks. In this period he can follow his whims with the bike, both in how much he does and how hard he rides. This period is very good for improving or learning technique, pedalling style and riding position. Even now you should still be following the rules of the sporting way of life. On no account should you suddenly stop training. If you can't face cycling, then by all means keep up your athletic condition by following any other sport which interests you. The more years a cyclist has trained, the more frequently he needs to train on the bike, and this holds good even for the transition period.

Mesocycles

Because of the way sporting development comes in phases, so the preparation and competition periods should be further broken down, in order that the training process can be better directed. Mesocycles embrace a period of three to six weeks. Correspondingly, one can distinguish between preparation, competition and intermediate mesocycles. In principle a mesocycle serves to suit the training load to increasing fitness. To this end, the volume of training (i.e., the distance) is first progressively increased, then towards the end of the mesocycle the intensity (the speed) is further built up. So, step by step, you move up to a higher performance level. Within the mesocycle the phases of upper-limit work should be alternated with recovery phases. In order to accelerate the adaptation processes of the body, it is often necessary, within the period of the mesocycle, to take the training load up to the limit. This is because the body reacts to meet the demands placed upon it. The make-up of a competition mesocycle preceding a major race is specially important. Three to five weeks before the event the training volume should be increased, and its intensity also gradually built up. Some two weeks before the event the training intensity should be increased still further, while the volume should slowly decrease.

Microcycles

Microcycles embrace a period of about one week. The make-up of a microcycle is very important, since you can only really concentrate on training if it can be viewed in distinct compartments. You must set yourself intermediate targets. The training plan covering one week consists of several training sessions with different types of work. Within this work the structure of the effort varies, that is the relationship between volume and intensity. Apart from this, the grade of effort changes — an easier training session will follow one of high intensity. By the proper constitution of the microcycles, the rider can be tested to the limit of his fitness at a given time. Between two such intensive training sessions you should insert one which aims at recovery. The best thing is to alternate an intensive, deeply fatiguing session with one which is more regenerative in character. If a rider gives up following microcycles and keeps training at the same rate, then first his improvement will cease, and soon he could even start to lose ground. Apart from this, unvarying training sessions always run the risk of monotony and staleness.

If you are training for speed and power, you need to be alert and psychologically keyed-up. For this reason any training sessions aimed at improving these qualities should be planned for days when condition is likely to be at a high level. When competition is included in the microcycle, it should be planned to fall during the overcompensation phase, which means that the last intensive and fatiguing session should fall some two or three days before the race. As the microcycle revolves around so many factors, it is always flexible and easy to vary, just as other outside conditions (races etc) and the rider's physical tolerance can also vary.

Planning and make-up of a training session

The training session forms the smallest planning unit of the whole training process. The sum of the single training sessions makes up the quality of the overall training programme. For this reason you should never train aimlessly, but be aware in every session of what it sets out to achieve and improve.

The individual training session will vary in duration according to the condition of the rider and the aim of the session (basic stamina, specific stamina, strength, speed, speed stamina, strength stamina). But generally it will last between one and six hours.

It is best to split the session into three parts:

☐ Preparation.

☐ Main section.

☐ Wind-down.

A week's training plan:

General guidelines

Monday:	Regenerative training (active recuperation): medium volume, low intensity; include some technique training.
Tuesday:	Intensive long-duration training with long intervals, for basic stamina, speed and strength stamina.
Wednesday:	Training for basic stamina: high volume, low intensity. Concurrent technique training.
Thursday:	Speed-oriented stamina training: high volume, high intensity; medium gears with high pedalling rate, interspersed with long and medium interval work.
Friday:	Regenerative training: high volume, low intensity. Technique training.
Saturday:	Work on basic and strength stamina: medium volume, high intensity, big gears. Alternatively a race.
Sunday:	Intensive long-duration training: high volume, high intensity. Alternatively a race.

For riders who have progressed to top level, I have put together the training plan on the following page with the aid of national road coach Karl Ziegler.

A week's training plan:

Guidelines for high-performance training

Monday:	Morning, easy stamina training (low gears). Afternoon, 2–3 hours' regeneration training.
Tuesday:	Morning, anaerobic training (1½–2 hours). Afternoon, easy stamina training, aerobic (2–3 hours).
Wednesday:	Long-distance training (180–220km), aerobic, stripped for racing.
Thursday:	Intensive long-distance training with changes of rhythm (aerobic, anaerobic surges).
Friday:	Morning, easy regeneration training (2 hours). Afternoon, easy distance training (2–3 hours), low gears.
Saturday:	Easy riding (1½–2 hours). Race preparation, trying-out of equipment.

Preparation

During the preparation part of a training session the rider should work on his suppleness and flexibility, joints and muscles, by using low gears. This preparation effort warms up the body, sets the circulation moving faster; the capillaries swell, improving the blood supply and slightly increasing the body temperature. At the same time you get into your best pedalling rhythm. Once these details are seen to, you can start increasing the intensity of the training effort.

As well as putting the body into the best state to accept the demands of training, this preparation period is important to achieve concentration on the training to come. This positive fixing of the sights on training increases its effectiveness. The rider must be clear in his mind what is the goal of the training session, what kind of effort is expected of him, and why he is making it. Lastly, he should be aware of how this training session fits into the overall plan. The rider should concentrate on the main exercise of the session. This mental and physical preparation for the main part of the training session should last some 15 to 30 minutes.

Main part

In the main part of the training session exercises are performed which, based on the training plan, will serve either to develop or consolidate the rider's fitness. Conditional elements are improved, as well as technique and tactics, and every so often the rider's progress is tested and checked. It has been proved that training exercises which demand mental freshness and concentration should be scheduled for the first half of the main part of the session. Such exercises are:

☐ Development of speed and power.

☐ Sprint practice.

☐ Improvement of maximum strength.

☐ Work on technique and riding action.

In the second half of the main part the real stamina training should be planned. If you practised sprinting during this half you would not be so much improving the sprinting as the speed stamina which would be necessary in finishes. You could devote the whole of the session towards basic or competition-specific stamina, or plan several different types of exercise within one training session. Clearly this latter course makes the session more interesting, staves off the effect of fatigue and allows a greater overall work volume. However, every training session should concentrate on one aspect, even if it introduces others. The art of structuring a training session lies in finding a compromise between complete concentration on one aspect and providing a variety of different training exercises.

Wind-down

The wind-down is a very important aspect of a training session. Already this part of the session sees the start of regeneration, in the sense of active recovery. The quicker you can recover, the quicker the next training session can follow on. In the wind-down the muscles start to ease out, and the nervous tension is released. The

cardio-vascular circulation and the body's energy transport systems start moving towards a resting state. In particular, the lactic acid produced as a result of high-intensity effort is broken down completely. This is done by changing down to lowish gears and letting the legs spin easily. You can sit up, even take your hands off the bars, and breathe deeply, easing as you do so the muscles of the back. It is just as important to recuperate mentally, let all the tensions drain away and be glad that you have had a fruitful session. A training session shouldn't suddenly come to an end. It should be followed by a period of assessment; have the planned efforts and exercises in fact been carried out satisfactorily? The training effect is higher if the rider involves himself with the theory of the plan as well as the practice. For this reason the weighing-up process after each session is important.

You can see in the structure of a training session of any seriously pursued sport — and cycling in particular — how much personal commitment it demands from the sportsman. His individual peak performance can only be reached

if every training session is properly structured.

Checking your performance progress

Top-flight sportsmen should check their progress about once every two months — after each mesocycle, in fact. A proven increase in performance levels gives added stimulus to subsequent training. It also serves to establish the effort structure (intensity and volume) for the next mesocycle. For as fitness increases, so the intensity and volume of the subsequent training must also be increased, in order to achieve continual progress. In cycling you can measure fitness progress through the following methods:

☐ By covering a test course (say 5km) at maximum speed.

☐ By ergometer tests.

☐ By success in certain races.

The test course
The best test course should be on quiet, preferably flat, roads. It could be 5km long. You can measure its distance with a

cyclometer or a car odometer, or simply use the distance stones on many roads. For this 5km time trial you should be physically fresh, fully concentrated, and already warmed-up. Everything must be done to ensure that the time achieved is the best possible one. You can reckon the average speed by the following formula:

$$\text{Speed in kph} = \frac{\text{Distance (metres)}}{\text{Time (seconds)}} \times 3.6$$

The resulting speed worked out represents the top performance at that moment. In the following table the times and corresponding speeds for a 5km test course are shown:

Speed (kph)	Time (min/sec)
30	10.00
31	9.41
32	9.23
33	9.05
34	8.49
35	8.34
36	8.20
37	8.06
38	7.54
39	7.42

Speed (kph)	Time (min/sec)
40	7.30
41	7.19
42	7.09
43	6.59
44	6.49
45	6.40
46	6.31
47	6.23
48	6.15
49	6.07
50	6.00

The ergometer effort test

Regular ergometer tests are the best way for a sportsman to establish his condition relative to a specific sports discipline. The riding position should approximate to the position on the bike. Effort tests for the cyclist begin at a setting of 150 watts (100 for women) and this level is raised every three minutes by 50 watts. This is continued until the maximum effort load is reached. In certain special tests a lactic acid level is measured from a blood sample taken from the earlobe just as the end of each effort level is reached. The better the rider's stamina, the higher the level of effort at which the lactic acid levels start to increase. It is important in estimating the intensity levels of the next part of the training process to know when the lactic acid reading reaches the level of 4mmol/l, the aerobic-anaerobic threshold at which one type of effort becomes the other. The pulse rate which is measured at that particular load level is the pulse rate at which one can then achieve the maximal training effect. So we can see that the optimal training intensity is determined by the heart rate at this threshold. But even without this specialized testing, one can establish from experience what is one's optimal training intensity, and I will explain this a little later.

Racing successes

Ultimately the experienced rider or his trainer can tell from his results in road races, time trials, track races, and so on whether, and by how much, his condition has improved. It becomes clear in racing, and on the day after, how much effort tolerance has increased. The better the race performances, and the greater the effort tolerance, the greater the intensity and volume of subsequent training, always taking into account the ultimate goal of the training plan.

Checking optimal training loads

We should first differentiate between the region of intensive training, which demands between 80 and 100 per cent of maximum effort, and the region of extensive training, which demands 60 to 80 per cent. The shorter the training course, the more intensively it must be tackled, and vice versa: the longer the training distance, the less intensively (and more extensively) it can be ridden, in order to achieve the desired training effect. Training with an intensity of less than 60 per cent of maximum is not effective. It is simply pottering about. But it does aid active recovery. Training sessions with intensive and extensive training loads, and those which serve recovery, should be alternated. Since to achieve continual improvement your training will require frequent efforts to the limit of your capabilities, you must know where those limits lie, and to

this purpose there are three different points of reference:

☐ The aerobic-anaerobic threshold.
☐ The heart rate.
☐ Fatigue.

The aerobic-anaerobic threshold

This value must first be established through special tests on the ergometer. It lies at levels which are low for the rider with little stamina training behind him, and increases with the rider's stamina.
When the stamina level is very high indeed, the lactic acid deposits start to show at such high levels of effort that the point of aerobic-anaerobic transition (4mmol/l of lactic acid in the blood) cannot be used as a measurement for training intensity. However, for most riders this aerobic-anaerobic threshold, or the pulse rate which matches it, has been proved a very good training rate. With good stamina-trained riders this threshold occurs when the pulse rate is about 160–180.

Heart rate

Even if you have no knowledge of the aerobic-anaerobic threshold, the heart rate can be used as a very good measurement of the intensity of training. When training loads are intensive the rate generally lies between 160 and 180. When the training loads are only extensive, the rate is between 140 and 160. On long training runs you should ride at a speed which takes the rate up to the 140–160 level, a speed which you should then be able to maintain. This speed should work out between 60 and 80 per cent of the speed achieved over your 5km test course. On short training bursts you can work at 160–180 beats per minute, which should be at 80 to

The heart rate as a measurement of optimal training intensity in relation to age.

Age	Max. heart rate (220 − age)	Optimal training heart rate
20	200	175–185
25	195	170–180
30	190	165–175
35	185	160–170
40	180	155–165

100 per cent of that maximum test course speed.

Fatigue

You can also base your effort level on the appearance of fatigue, and on the time it takes you to recover completely. A training effort is most effective if it produces extreme tiredness. Fatigue after optimal training efforts is characterized by weakness in muscles, loss of concentration, and a generally lowered level of activity. Nightly rest should not, however, suffer; if this happens after a training effort to the limit, then a regenerative-type training session should always be introduced. The next morning the pulse rate should have calmed down to something like the normal resting pulse rate. Efforts to the limit should be attempted less frequently by developing riders (juniors and schoolboys). Such flat-out efforts are produced by training-loads of simultaneously high volume and high intensity. Frequent efforts of this kind can, however, lead to symptoms of overtraining, even with very advanced riders. Training efforts, fatigue and regeneration must be

harmoniously balanced to bring about an optimal increase in performance in the long term.

Regeneration

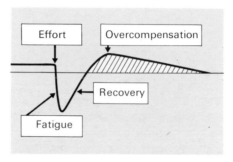

A new and demanding training session should only take place when the important functional systems of the body (energy sources, acid levels, nervous and hormonal regulation systems) have recovered. The improvement in fitness as a result of a training session is called overcompensation. The quicker the body's recovery, therefore, the more frequently you can train. The more frequent the training sessions, the quicker and greater the improvement in sporting condition. Regeneration processes are already beginning while the training effort is being made, and they work even harder

during the wind-down phase of training. The processes leading to recovery and recuperation improve together with the body's ability to adapt to increasing effort. Therefore a possible measure of training effort can be the time needed for the recuperation process.

You can read exhaustion on this rider's face.

Signs of fatigue under varying efforts

	Low fatigue (low effort)	Deep fatigue (optimal effort)	Very deep fatigue (limit effort)	Symptoms after limit effort
Skin colour	Faint colouring	Strong colouring	Very strong colouring or striking paleness	Paleness for several days
Sweat secretion	According to temperature, light to medium	Heavy	Very heavy	Night sweating
Quality of movement	In control	Beginning to make mistakes	Strong disturbance of co-ordination, weak movement	Weak and unco-ordinated in subsequent training
Concentration	Normal	Lack of attention to explanations, less receptive to challenges of technical and tactical nature	Considerably lowered concentration, nervousness, carelessness	Lack of attention, unable to concentrate on tasks requiring mental application
General state	No problems	Muscle weakness, breathing difficulties, strengthlessness, lowering of performance	Leaden muscles, muscle and joint pain, giddiness, sickness, burning in the chest	Disturbed sleep, lack of strength, continuing muscle and joint pains
State of effort-readiness	Continuous	Lowered activity. Desire for longer breaks	Desire for complete rest and cessation of training	No wish to restart training the next day. Resistance to the demands of the trainer. Indifference
Disposition	Content, uplifted	Somewhat affected, but still content	Contrary, obstructive, aggressive	Depressed; doubtful about value of training; seeking reasons to stay off training

The time necessary for the recuperation of the various functional systems is different. But by taking regenerative measures this time can be shortened. The measures are as follows:

Nutrition	Carbohydrate
	Fats
	Protein
	Electrolytes
	Water
	Vitamins
Relaxation	Sleep
	Gentle training
	Change of surroundings
	Sedatives
Physical steps	Massage
	Baths
	Sauna
	Change of climate
	Altitude
Training build-up	Stamina training
	Speed
	Strength
	Technique
	Co-ordination

In **nutrition** it is particularly important to replace the carbohydrate source, the minerals and liquid lost in sweat, and the vitamins, as quickly as possible. In terms of **relaxation** proper sleep is as vital as leading a healthy sporting life. Gentle training can ease nervous tension. If you have become stale or overtrained a change of surroundings can be fruitful. Mild sedatives may be worthwhile if sleep is elusive for some time.

Such **physical means** as massage, relaxing baths, contrast baths, saunas and high-altitude sunshine can be a great support. For example, between two training sessions a massage speeds recovery, so high training loads can be imposed in a shorter time. Even altitude training can help regeneration and the lifting of performance.

The optimal application by the rider of proper **training build-up** aids recovery. It has been shown that in modern high-performance training the degree of awareness by the rider plays a great role in performance improvement and in regeneration. The use of microcycles and mesocycles should guarantee the recovery of the body between training sessions by the application of rhythmic physical demands in the training process. Exercise and the results of training should be so

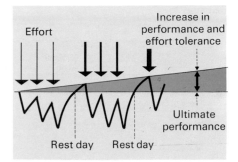

measured that recuperation is ensured via active recovery. Training practice has, however, shown us that with advanced well-trained riders it is not always necessary to await complete recuperation before beginning a new training session. It is sometimes worthwhile to provoke a much deeper fatigue by several intensive sessions in succession. For example, you can have three intensive sessions to limit effort following one another and then slip in a rest day, as some professionals do (see illustration).

Overtraining

By overtraining we mean the drop in a rider's performance over a long period, as opposed to the short-lived fatigue which is normal after training efforts. In fact, overtraining is less the result of too much training than of mis-training. It happens when the loads imposed by training are too great in relation to the tolerance of the rider. It is perhaps better to talk of the overdemand syndrome.

The rider has to react not only to the loads imposed in training, but also to those imposed by his work, his studies, schoolwork, family, and so on. Such outside influences can temporarily reduce the effort tolerance of the rider, and if in such cases the training structure is strictly maintained, then what is normally an optimal effort becomes a maximum effort — to the limit — from which he can recover only slowly. If the training plan is adhered to, despite the rider's lowered state, then after some time he will enter into a state of long-term fatigue. He will not be able to recover after a training session, and so his condition falls inexorably away. Since the signs of overtraining manifest themselves principally through the involuntary nervous systems, we have differentiated between two forms of overtraining according to the main symptoms. These two forms are called the sympathetic and parasympathetic forms.

Sympathetic overtraining
This is a condition in which the excitement processes predominate. The organism can no longer switch from the condition of excitement (ruled by the sympathetic nervous system) to one of rest (ruled by the parasympathetic nervous system). This form of overtraining comes about specially when the body is subject to too high an intensity of training load, without the foundation for such loads being laid by an appropriate volume of training. Beginners and relatively untrained riders frequently get into this condition when they follow

Symptoms and signs to differentiate the two forms of overtraining	
Sympathetic overtraining	Parasympathetic overtraining
Slight fatigue	Abnormal fatigue
Sleep disturbed Appetite curbed Weight loss	Sleep undisturbed Appetite slightly curbed Weight maintained or varying
Sweating, night sweating, hot or cold hands	Normal temperature
Headache, feeling of unease, heart pains, heart pounding, resting heart rate speeds up	Circulation tests at low loads give a normal result, but at high loads are atypical, often showing high blood pressure
Low powers of recovery	Good, frequently very good powers of recovery
Inner uneasiness, loss of drive, listlessness, depression, discontent	Inner calm, measurable loss of drive, normal condition, contentment, indifference

their own enthusiasm and do too much too soon, such as overloading themselves in short-duration training, or taking part in races too soon.

Parasympathetic overtraining

This is a condition in which the inhibiting processes predominate. The organism cannot change from the condition of rest (nervus parasympathicus) to one of excitement (nervus sympathicus). Nowadays this condition occurs far more frequently among high-performance sportsmen. It happens especially when the volume of training is too great, and above all when this is coupled with similar overdoses of intensity training.

When overtraining happens, not only the interplay between the two involuntary nervous systems is upset, but also the central nervous system and the hormonal system. Disturbances of these regulating systems reduce the rider's capabilities, in order to protect the peripheral cells from being overtaxed. The overtrained rider is irritable. He can show signs of hysteria, he grumbles and is contrary. Sometimes there is belligerence and an inability to take any criticism. But other signs of overtraining are increasing phlegmaticism and a loss of drive. Other possibilities are listlessness, an unsettled feeling, insecurity and a tendency towards depression and melancholia. The fall-off in performance relates above all to the strongly developed qualities (strength, speed, endurance). Recovery times lengthen. Any 'snap' is gone. The style is lost, the smooth pedalling style is disturbed. In races the overtrained rider tends to give up when the going gets tough, or doesn't contest the final sprint. Normal tactical principles are forgotten. Gradually a real fear of racing develops. Characteristically, the sympathetically overtrained rider feels that he is unable to meet a challenge, whereas the parasympathetically overtrained rider feels fit, and in fact can manage quite large volumes of training (long distances) without noticeable tiredness. But he has lost the ability to ride at high speeds, and for this reason he usually finishes road races in the main bunch, or even at the back, but without feeling exhausted. He feels that he could even ride the race all over again. He usually does not notice that all his competitive spirit and edge have disappeared.

There are also accompanying physical disturbances, such as restless sleep, affected appetite, coupled with weight loss. The bowel-stomach function is upset, and frequently there are headaches (especially with the sympathetically overtrained) and sweating attacks. The overtrained rider also tends to pick up infections easily, because the body's normal defence systems are reduced.

Thus it can be seen that overtraining results from mistakes in the training plan, and that overtraining can cause problems in the rider's way of life and his health.

Treatment of overtraining

Overtraining isn't a sickness. But if any rider thinks he is overtrained, he should seek a medical check-up. Health problems which might have caused the situation should be identified and tackled. Even a simple infection or a decaying tooth can help the onset of overtraining. You must also be

Possible reasons for the onset or exacerbation of overtraining

Main mistakes in training	Factors which can diminish performance		
	Way of life	*Circumstances*	*Health problems*
Recovery has been neglected	Unenriching sleep	Family tensions	Feverish colds
Training loads increased too quickly	Irregular daily programme	Unhappy in job	Stomach trouble
Too quick increase in training loads after enforced breaks (injury, illness)	Dissipated way of life	Too much work, study	Chronic infection (tonsils, sinuses, teeth)
Too great a volume of submaximal and maximal efforts	Alcohol and nicotine	Continual fight against 'unsporting' surroundings (family, superiors)	After-effects of infections (tonsillitis, scarlet fever, etc)
Too high an intensity in long-distance efforts during stamina training	Too much caffeine		
Too great a concentration on technical improvements without active recuperation	Bad living conditions	Distractions (TV, cinema)	
	Lack of free time or badly-spent free time (no relaxation)		
Too many races	Bad diet		
Too much concentration on one type of training	Pace of life too fast		
Mistaken confidence in trainer. More and more misfortunes because of targets set too high			

sure that there is no infection of the heart muscle causing the fall-off in performance. The principle in treating overtraining is the elimination of the causes. It is also important to restore the rider's confidence, by explaining how harmless the condition is. It would be the greatest mistake to try 'strong-arm methods', by increasing the training load. The result would be the opposite to the one sought. It would be just as wrong to order the rider to take a complete rest. The sudden release from effort would just cause more trouble. The right method is to reduce the load and substitute some recuperative measures. No checks on condition through races or test courses should be made for quite a while.

The sympathetic form of overtraining can usually be overcome in one or two weeks. The parasympathetic form is more problematical. It normally lasts. Typically, it can last several weeks or months before you can start thinking of racing again. It is often worth dropping one complete competition period. The danger otherwise is that the rider may come to terms with his lessened ability, lose interest and quit the sport entirely. At the very least the rider should have a six-week period of highly-varied training, with a reduction in

Treatment of overtraining

	When the excitement processes predominate	When the inhibiting processes predominate
Diet	Stimulate the appetite, leaning towards basic foods (milk, fruit, vegetables) and reduce protein Cut out stimulants (caffeine) Take a vitamin course, above all B and C vitamins	Favour acid foods (meat, cheese, eggs, cereals) Vitamin course (B and C)
Physical therapy	Open-air swimming. Bath in the evening (with relaxing bath salts). Cold wash or shower in the mornings, followed by brisk rub-down. Relaxing massage Relaxing exercises	Contrast baths and contrast showers. Medium-heat sauna with several cold showers. Deep massage. Intensive gym work with power exercises
Climatic therapy	Change of surroundings to a calm place (woodland, low mountains). Avoid intensive sunlight, but slight ultra-violet treatment possible	Seek stimulating climate, particularly coastal

volume and intensity. The load should very gradually be increased again, until the original level is reached once more. Then first the volume and then the intensity of the training load should be built up. While this corrective training is taking place, dietary measures, physical and climatic therapy can also be applied.

Prevention of overtraining

It is better to avoid overtraining than have to treat it, so here are some measures to prevent it happening.

1. Good training foundations. First build up a high measure of basic stamina and only then start to think of increasing the intensity. Rational planning, organization and periodization of training.
2. Sufficient recovery allowed before the beginning of a new training session, above all after a session of high load.
3. Regular (daily) and twelve-months-a-year training, with periods of high load alternating with those of less effort.
4. Attention to factors which favour the onset of overtraining, i.e. which reduce the effort tolerance of the rider. Suit the training load to the changing effort tolerance of the rider.
5. A varied construction of training, avoiding monotony and stereotyping.
6. Leading a sporting way of life.
7. Keeping a training diary, learning to observe your own progress, having regular checks by sports doctors.
8. A trusting collaboration between rider, trainer and sports doctor.

High training loads in training alone are enough to stimulate the desired adaptation processes of the body, and as a rule do not lead to overtraining. But any extra stress can favour its onset. Such an additional stress for a roadman would be, for example, the heat. It imposes a climatic stress which is frequently underestimated.

Sweating, consequent liquid and mineral losses, increased use of and loss of vitamin C, together with high exertion, can produce exhaustion.

Road riders have differing tolerances to heat. Riders who know that they have low resistance when events are run off in heat are anxious about even starting in hot conditions. Such riders should take care to do their training in cooler conditions. In addition, when it is hot, such riders should reduce their training volume, allowing some increase in intensity. It is especially important during hot periods to have a vitamin-rich diet, including a good intake of vitamin C. Attention should also be paid to replacing lost body liquid and minerals (common salt, calcium, iron, magnesium, potassium). Regular checks on body weight give early warning of problems with mineral and liquid deficiencies, as well as in the energy balance.

Training in reverse — acute release syndrome

The adaptation of the body to effort basically doesn't happen in only one direction. The function and structure of organs, organ systems and the body as a whole, can be thought of as a co-operative. Just as skills and abilities can be perfected or improved through training, so they can deteriorate if they are not trained. The process of adaptation to a lower performance level brings with it a comprehensive series of changes throughout the whole body, but especially in the involuntary nervous systems. The interruption of training can trigger off in a sportsman all sorts of problems, which we recognize as the acute release syndrome. The problems following abrupt cessation of training are more manifold at higher training levels. The reasons which persuade or compel riders to cease or reduce training are many and varied, for example accidents (concussion), injuries, sickness, or personal reasons. Inactivity and a lack of training result, after a delay of two to ten days, in the following disturbances in about 80 per cent of highly-trained roadmen (a lower percentage with trackmen).

☐ Feeling of pressure and stitch in the heart area.

☐ Extra heart beats.

☐ Giddiness, headaches, circulation problems.

☐ Feeling of fullness in the stomach, digestion problems.

☐ Disturbed sleep, upset appetite.

☐ Feeling of unrest. Tendency to break out in perspiration.

☐ Weariness.

☐ Depression, lack of drive.

☐ Lack of concentration. Slow reactions.

☐ Unstable mental condition.

Symptoms relating to the heart are felt in about 95 per cent of cases, which is not surprising, since the heart is the organ most affected by the training process. It is totally wrong for a highly-trained sportsman to stop all activity, particularly if he has been trained for stamina — as a road rider, for example.

Even after injury it is advisable to try to maintain training condition for as long as possible by exercising the sound limbs. Using isometric exercises, heavy massage, water and electrotherapies, even a bed-ridden sportsman can stave off the onset of acute release syndrome. In fact sportsmen who do develop this syndrome usually have a good idea what is wrong, and spontaneously develop a driving urge to get back to activity as soon as possible. Many sportsmen who have to cease training suddenly because of professional or private reasons, feel really ill. They go from doctor to doctor until someone gives them the advice they want — namely, to start training again. Complete rest for such sportsmen is totally the wrong advice.

Once a high-performance athlete has accustomed himself, through years of well-planned build-up training, to a certain level of performance, then it is impossible to adapt to the low output level of a sedentary life within a matter of days without some disturbances taking place. People don't often realize this.

The principle of **training in reverse,** or training down, is much too little known. The problems which can strike sportsmen suddenly released from their accustomed training load are often used by non-sportsmen as an argument against sport itself. But such problems don't strike every trained athlete, and they are, in any case, easily cured by simple means. It is enough to take away the training load gradually instead of suddenly. Carrying on training at 30 to 50 per cent of the normal level is sufficient. The sportsman can even switch to another sport, such as long-distance running, for instance. The process of training down should be planned to last one or two years. The psychological side should not be neglected either. You must realize how the rider who is training down is moving away from a life in which sport played a major role. The phase of training down should include very healthy pursuits, those which really everyone should follow. It should include stamina training — not necessarily on the bike — for about an hour, at least twice a week, using the age-related pulse-rate as a check. This healthy training should continue throughout a lifetime, in order to maintain fitness and health. Just as with building up performance levels, so with taking them down, the same principle applies: do it gradually.

Nutrition

If a rider is to reach and maintain his potential, then an appropriate and effective diet is essential. During the regeneration phases of training the body must replace all the substances which, during the previous effort, it has used up or otherwise lost. But in nature there is no single food which contains all the materials necessary to life in the right proportions. So the body must have a varied bill of fare for its

Taking in nourishment

nourishment. In the interests of maintaining his own condition, the rider should not follow an exclusive diet, but one which is varied and worthwhile. Proper nourishment must fulfil the following conditions:

☐ The increased **energy demand** created by effort must be matched by a corresponding increase in energy intake.

☐ The **balance between nutrients** must be maintained in the same way as training is balanced (for stamina, strength, etc).
☐ Because of the increased consumption of protein, carbohydrate and fat, the **vitamin demand** so created must be satisfied in a balanced way.
☐ **Minerals and trace elements,** used up by increased enzyme activity and lost in sweat, must be replaced adequately and in the right proportions.
☐ The **fluid** lost as a result of the body's temperature-regulation systems must be replaced to the required degree, always maintaining the right mineral balance in the replacement of the liquid.

A good balance sheet of nutrition should satisfy all these five requirements. So good nutrition is not just a matter of replacing energy, but also of replacing substances which in themselves do not provide energy (vitamins, minerals, trace elements, water) but through their presence allow the metabolism to function properly. The aim should be to replace everything in a balanced way.

159

Energy demand

The unit of measurement for the consumption of energy, and also for the energy content of a nutrient is the Calorie. One Calorie (Cal) is the amount of heat needed to warm one litre of water from 14.5°C to 15.5°C. An expert committee of the World Health Organization also decreed (as from January 1, 1978) that the world-wide unit of energy, work and heat should be the joule. In nutrition, one Calorie equals 4.1868 joules, or one joule equals 0.2388 Calories. Nutrients have the following calorific values:

> One gram of carbohydrate can provide 17.2 joules (4.1 Cal).
> One gram of protein can provide 17.2 joules (4.1 Cal).
> One gram of fat can provide 38.9 joules (9.3 Cal).

When it comes to meeting energy demands, it is not just a matter of the quantity of nutrients consumed, but also the composition of the nutrition — its quality. In relation to its calorific value 1g of fat equals 2.27g of carbohydrate or protein, but the protein has more importance for building tissue. Not all forms of nutrients are good for energy provision, indeed some work in a totally opposite direction.

What nutrients should be used for energy provision really depends on the circumstances in which energy is required. We have already written on distinguishing three separate forms of energy providers, from which above all two forms, carbohydrate and fat (which can be completely burnt up in the energy process), are most important for stamina (aerobic energy provision).

Aerobic energy, produced under full oxygen supply, consists of the complete breaking-down of the nutrients, mainly carbohydrates and fat, which has end products of carbon dioxide and water. When efforts are very high to maximal, then carbohydrate is the preferred energy source, with fat being preferred at low and medium effort levels.

The different forms of energy production are necessary in order to satisfy the energy demand in the best ways according to changing conditions. In road racing the daily energy requirement for intensive energy demand is an average 24,300 J (5,800 Cal), while in track racing it is an average 21,800 J (5,200 Cal).

Eddy Merckx, according to medical research, had an hourly consumption of some 6,700 J (1,600 Cal) during a circuit race, which means during a three-hour event he would burn up 20,100 J (4,800 Cal). Professional road riders would use up something like 33,500 J (8,000 Cal) during a stage of the Tour de France. In a 300-kilometre single-day event, the consumption could be 43,500 J (10,400 Cal).

The upper limit of food consumption that the digestive system can cope with in a day is around 25,000 J (6,000 Cal). In comparison, a normal adult with a sedentary job would use 9,200 J (2,200 Cal) per day. A medium-level physical workman would have a demand of 11,700 J (2,800 Cal) while a heavy workman would need 16,700 J (4,000 Cal).

Over long periods, energy supply and demand balance out. The most important yardstick on whether this is so is body weight. A constant body weight in a well-trained sportsman is a sign of good energy balance. For this reason the weight should be checked every day, especially during periods of heavy training.

The right composition of nutrition

If your diet is to allow you to perform well, it must have the right nutrients in the correct proportions, replacing the energy consumed. Food must be properly chosen with this, and the efforts to come, in mind. The main distinction in nutrition between the leisure sportsman and the dedicated sportsman is that mistakes in nutrition weigh heavier with the latter.

Carbohydrates
Each of us, during a 70-year life span, consumes more than six tons of carbohydrates. From your diet carbohydrates provide 50 to 60 per cent of energy requirements.
The principal sources of carbohydrate are bread, cakes, potatoes, rice, pasta, fruit, honey, sugar, marmalade and porridge oats.
These can be split into simple and composite carbohydrates. The most important simple carbohydrate is glucose. What we normally call sugar is sucrose (cane or beet sugar), a double sugar which has one molecule of glucose and one of fructose. The central nervous system — the brain and the spinal cord — can exist almost completely on glucose. For this reason it is important to maintain a constant blood sugar level. Certain by-products of carbohydrate metabolism are also important to nutrition, so some carbohydrate is needed every day, some 100–120g being regarded as the minimum requirement.
The stored form of the body's carbohydrate is glycogen, which is laid down in the muscles and the liver.

The 'hunger knock'
The stored liver glycogen has the task of regulating blood sugar levels. Muscle glycogen, however, serves as a direct energy source for the working muscles. If through a bodily dysfunction, or through a poor ability to take up oxygen under effort (as happens with a poorly-trained sportsman) the blood sugar level starts to fall, the effect on the central nervous system is what the cyclist has come to call 'hunger knock'. After training for only one or two hours the undertrained rider will start to tremble, go into a cold sweat, become unsteady on his machine, and develop a craving for something to eat, preferably something sweet. The central nervous system is reacting to the lowered blood sugar with alarm systems, feeling itself threatened. These systems effectively rule out any form of good physical performance, since the body is concentrating on lifting the blood sugar level to its right point. This condition can be quickly cured by taking just a small amount of carbohydrate, say a couple of sugar lumps, some dried fruit, a slice of bread and so on. With highly-trained sportsmen the regulating systems of using carbohydrates and fats for energy are so well developed that such a situation rarely ever happens.

Muscle glycogen: the body's carbohydrate store

Carbohydrates are important energy-providers for every sporting effort. Anaerobic efforts, efforts produced without using oxygen, such as power efforts in track sprinting, are only possible through the burning of carbohydrates. Carbohydrates are also necessary for all intensive stamina efforts, be they short-duration stamina efforts (the kilometre time trial), medium-duration efforts (team pursuit) or long-duration efforts (road racing). For road racing we can state that whoever has the greatest carbohydrate reserves at the decisive point, assuming equal fitness, then he will do better.

The size of the carbohydrate reserves, held in the form of glycogen in the muscles and liver, is an important limiting factor of performance. Normally these reserves are around 300–400g, corresponding to an energy reserve of 5,000 to 6,700 J (1,200–1,600 Cal). The better the carbohydrate store is filled, the more easily these reserves can be mobilized. Carbohydrates, specially the muscle glycogen stores, are expensive energy reserves, which can only be used to a limited degree, and which are therefore used sparingly in normal life.

How can the carbohydrate store be preserved?

As well as burning up carbohydrates for energy, the body can draw upon fats for the same purpose. Unlike carbohydrates, the body's fat stores are virtually inexhaustible. In a normal adult, they can provide some 210,000 J (50,000 Cal). If one can persuade the body to burn predominantly fats, then the carbohydrate stores are preserved. You can best train the body to metabolise fat by having a good diet, and by training long distances on low to medium gears. Consequently the body tends to go to the fat stores for energy during races whenever the pace eases. You should always eat carbohydrates before and during the race, so that the body has enough carbohydrate stores for the decisive phase of the race.

How can the carbohydrate store be increased?

There is a special readiness to replenish muscle glycogen during the first ten hours following an exhausting effort. Normally with a usual diet it would take more than five days to bring the carbohydrate reserve levels back to their previous mark, but taking carbohydrate-rich food brings that period down to two days. If, after an exhausting long-distance effort you take a carbohydrate-rich diet for three days, then the carbohydrate reserves can be built up to 1½ or 2 times normal. For the cyclist then, this means an exhausting outing four days before the target race, and a carbohydrate-rich diet for three days prior to the event. This would mean going to the start line with reserves of 700–800g, that is 11,700 to 13,400 J (2,800–3,200 Cal). Against otherwise equal opponents you will have an advantage.

Fats

Fats consist of glycerin and fatty acids. There are saturated fats and unsaturated fats. Certain unsaturated fats are vital for the metabolism, and are thus described as essential fats. In normal nutrition fats provide more than 40 per cent of energy.

The main fat sources are meat, butter, margarine, milk and dairy products, eggs, bread and nuts. With fats come the fat-soluble vitamins: A, D, E, K. Fats have many advantages. They can be highly saturated into a low volume of food, and give a diet variety and taste. Fat makes eating more enjoyable, so the tendency towards fat-rich foods is understandable. The trouble is that a fat-rich diet tends to limit sporting performances, because more oxygen is needed to consume fats for energy. The sportsman's diet must be low in fat to allow more room for protein and carbohydrate. The amount of fat energy should be no more than 30 per cent of a sportsman's energy intake.

In order to keep down to this level, it is best to avoid animal fats, but also to cut down on cheese, cakes, tarts and sweets (chocolate contains 30 per cent fat!), sauces, mayonnaise, eggs, pancakes, chips, crisps and any battered dishes. Nevertheless, the body's own metabolism of fat, maintained subcutaneously, remains the principal form of energy supply, especially for any event requiring long-term efforts of low intensity.

Protein

Protein is the building material of the human organism. Protein is made up of amino acids, containing oxygen, hydrogen, nitrogen and carbon, as well as other elements such as sulphur and phosphorus. In all there are some 20 different amino acids, which combine in different ways to form the body's tissues, cells, organs, enzymes, hormones and antibodies. Through their build-up into enzymes and hormones the proteins are indirectly involved in the body's metabolism. Through the construction of antibodies they are also involved in the body's defences against infection. The main protein sources in nutrition are meat, milk and dairy products, eggs, fish and bread. As the body cannot store protein, the body must have a regular daily intake of high-value protein foods.

The biological values of protein
Just as the human body needs different proteins from other animal or vegetable organisms, so the biological worth of various proteins is also different. The biological value of a protein food is decided by the number of grams of body protein that can be taken from 100g of the given food. In general animal protein has a higher value than vegetable protein (see table). However, different proteins of low value can combine to give a higher value than an individual animal protein. Such combinations are mixtures of beans and maize, milk and wheat, milk and oats, egg and wheat, egg and milk and also egg and potatoes. So not just the amount, but also the selection of proteins is important. By correct mixing of protein sources, one could even eliminate meat from the sportsman's diet.

Protein and effort

Protein should make up about 15 to 20 per cent of a sportsman's energy diet, split equally between animal and vegetable protein. When training is particularly stamina-oriented, then the protein supply can be at the lower limit, with the carbohydrate intake being correspondingly increased. With strength-oriented training, or sessions with high effort intensity, the protein level should be near the upper limit, and carbohydrate reduced. The daily intake of the racing cyclist should be 2.5 to 3.3g of protein per 1kg of body weight.

Vitamins

Vitamins are vital compounds which the body itself cannot produce. As components of enzymes and hormones they take part in many ways in the body's metabolic processes. The higher consumption of fat, carbohydrate and protein in the case of the sportsman requires intake of the vitamins appropriate to the various body processes involved in sport. If the high energy demand, in the case of top sportsmen around 21,000 J (5,000 Cal) daily, is fulfilled

Relative biological values of various types of protein for human beings

Egg		100	
Beef		92–96	Animal proteins
Fish		94	
Milk		88	
Cheese		85	
Soya		84	
Seaweed		81	
Rye		76	
Beans		72	
Rice		70	
Potato		70	Vegetable proteins
Bread		70	
Lentils		60	
Wheat		56	
Peas		56	
Maize		54	
Beans and maize	(52 + 48%)	101	
Milk and wheat	(75 + 25%)	105	
Egg and wheat	(68 + 32%)	118	Good mixtures of animal and vegetable proteins
Egg and milk	(71 + 29%)	122	
Egg and potato	(35 + 65%)	137	

through a balanced diet, then the increased vitamin needs are usually met. Yet it is easy to find deficiencies among top performers of vitamins B_1, B_2, Niacin and C, and sometimes also B_6 and E. It is easy to lose a lot of vitamins B_1 and C during food preparation.

The relationship between vitamin demand and supply for the endurance sportsman

	Need	Supply
B_1	4–8mg	1.9mg
B_2	4mg	2.9mg
Niacin	30mg	18 mg
C	500mg	244 mg

The danger is of vitamin deficiency, most frequently in the above vitamins.

Minerals and trace elements

Minerals are salts of which the body needs more than 100mg per day. They are of greatest importance in maintaining water and acid balance, but also work as catalysts and components in enzymes for the building of the body and its metabolism. They also have a great role in the stimulation of the muscles, the peripheral nerves, and the central nervous system.

Trace elements are salts of which only a few milligrams per day are needed. But they also play an important role in the enzyme actions.

The water balance

Water is absolutely necessary for all the metabolic processes of living beings. It is the transport and disposal system for all materials in cells. The body of a grown person consists of some 60 per cent water. If you lose 2 per cent of body weight in water, there is a marked fall-off in endurance. If you lose 6 per cent, then there are considerable disturbances in the body. Lose 12 per cent, and you die. The brain, liver and muscles have a specially high water content. The daily water demand for a human being is between 2.5 and 3.5 litres, according to physical activity and outside temperature. But a sportsman can lose between 5 and 10 litres per day.

Water has a special role in temperature regulation. The human body is like an incinerator working at 25 to 30 per cent effectiveness. In other words, as a result of all the various metabolic processes, only 25 to 30 per cent is turned into mechanical energy, the rest given off as heat. The body can either radiate this heat, or counter its effect in sweat. With 1 litre of sweat the body can rid itself of 2400 J (580 Cal). The lost body water should be put back in as quickly as possible. But since with the water of sweat there is also a loss of minerals, then these too must be replaced in the right proportion at the same time. Just taking pure water, lemonade, tea or Coca-Cola, only serves to dilute the remaining minerals still further and to more mineral loss, hence the so-called 'water poisoning'.

To replace this lost body fluid it is best to take fruit juice, fresh fruit, fruit jams or special mineral drinks. You must think of replacing not just common salt, but also calcium, potassium, magnesium and iron.

In principle the fluid should be replaced in small doses, and slightly warmed, in order not to upset the stomach. After a high level of perspiration loss, the production of stomach acids is lowered, and thus the action of the acids as a barrier against bacteria entering the intestines is diminished. The taking of cold drinks predisposes the sportsman to throat infections, catarrh and diarrhoea.

A cyclist's high-performance diet

An ideal sporting diet can increase the effectiveness of training and improve racing results. But the diet has to be right for the demands actually placed on the body. It must be right for the type of effort you have to make, and for the type of event in which you take part. These requirements are best fulfilled if you split the diet into phases which correspond to physical demands. In this way we can distinguish the following diet phases.

1. Nutrition in the training build-up phase, the basic diet of the sportsman.
2. Nutrition pre-event.
3. Nutrition during the event.
4. Nutrition following the event.

Training build-up phase

Road riders and even track riders (pursuiters, six-day riders, stayers) must first have good basic stamina. This is a matter of developing the red, slow-twitch muscle fibres by doing high training volumes at low or medium intensity. Adaptation to this quality shows itself biochemically in the optimalization of the fat metabolism process. Apart from doing plenty of fast pedalling in low gears, this quality development can be aided by the right diet. To start with, the stamina-oriented sportsman should be undernourished, in order that he should start to tap his own body fat reserves. A well-trained stamina sportsman is thin, with a hollow-cheeked look. The best measure of thickness in the subcutaneous fat layer is taken from the fat folds on the rear of the upper arm and above the shoulder-blade. A sportsman is considered thin, if these folds are no thicker than 6mm. It is best to take this measurement during the preparation phase, preferably in the early season training camp. To stand any chance, a rider should have at least 5000km in his legs before the first race. Only when this condition is fulfilled should the rider start to consider more intensive training, and bring to bear his special knowledge of diet. The basic diet should be healthy, completely efficient, high in carbohydrates and protein, but low in fat. Endurance sportsmen need a high carbohydrate intake, some 56 to 60 per cent of the energy diet, and at the same time a high protein intake of some 17 per cent, corresponding to around 2.5g per kilogram of body weight. Power sportsmen (sprinters, kilometre riders etc) need a higher protein intake of some 18 to 20 per cent, corresponding to 2.5 to 3.3g per kilogram. Even road riders need to supplement their carbohydrate intake with a higher protein intake after intensive training loads. If you decide that increased protein is needed in such circumstances, then it is best taken in close proximity to the training effort, in order that the body can absorb the protein straight away into its structures. When selecting the kind of protein sources for the diet, it is better to go for lean products such as lean meat, low-fat cheese or cottage cheese, fish, so that the fat level stays low. The basic diet should be balanced to contain energy, nutrients, vitamins, minerals and fluids in the right proportions.

In particular, any sweat loss should be countered with a quick replacement of minerals and liquid.

The basic diet should also be a healthy one, with the highest possible content of fresh and 'live' foods, and as little as possible of foods which deliver only empty calories, such as products from white flour and sugar, fat and alcohol.

Pre-event phase
This phase is essentially one of filling up and if possible enlarging the body's glycogen store. To this end there should be an exhausting endurance training session three or four days before the race, in order to use up the current stores of glycogen. Then should follow three days of a carbohydrate-packed diet, with carbohydrate making up about 60 per cent of the energy food. Take care also to eat foods with a good content of vitamins B_1 and C, and potassium. Fluid and mineral losses should be balanced, to guard against muscle cramps during the event. This goes for road and track racing.

How energy food should be split up between various meals for power (track racing) and stamina (road racing).

	Power	Stamina
Breakfast	5900–6300 J (1400–1500 Cal)	5400–5900 J (1300–1400 Cal)
Elevenses	1700–2300 J (400– 550 Cal)	1700–2300 J (400– 550 Cal)
Lunch	5900–6300 J (1400–1500 Cal)	5000–5900 J (1200–1400 Cal)
Tea	1700–2100 J (400– 500 Cal)	2300–2500 J (550– 600 Cal)
Dinner	6300–8400 J (1500–2000 Cal)	6300–7500 J (1500–1800 Cal)

Average daily food needs for basic nutrition of a power sportsman (e.g. track rider) based on 23,000 J (5500 Cal), 20 per cent protein, 31 per cent fat, 49 per cent carbohydrate.

Meal	Food	Portion (g)	Energy content J	Cal
Breakfast	Milk	500	1250	300
	Cheese	30	290	70
	Meat	200	1670	400
	Egg	one egg	420	100
	Honey or marmalade	20	250	60
	Butter	20	630	150
	Fruit	150	420	100
	Bread	100	150	300
Elevenses	Malt coffee	–	–	–
	Milk	250	630	150
	Bread, biscuit	50	630	150
	Fruit/muesli	150	630	150
	Marmalade	30	290	70
Lunch	Soup	250	630	150
	Meat	200	2500	600
	Vegetables	200	630	150
	Potatoes	300	1050	250
	Stewed fruit	180	330	80
	Fruit	100	210	50
	Fruit or grape juice or milk	350	630	150

Meal	Food	Portion (g)	Energy content J	Energy content Cal
Tea	Tea with sugar	–	–	–
	Milk	250	630	150
	Cake	200	1250	300
	Cottage cheese	100	630	150
Dinner	Yoghurt	250	840	200
	Meat	100	840	200
	Sausage	50	540	130
	Cottage or other cheese	100	420	100
	Egg	one egg	420	100
	Fish	100	920	220
	Vegetables	200	420	100
	Butter	20	630	150
	Bread	250	2720	650
	Stewed fruit or juice or milk	– 200	– 330	– 80

Average daily food needs for an endurance sportsman (e.g. road rider) based on 23,000 J (5500 Cal), 15 per cent protein, 27 per cent fat, 58 per cent carbohydrate.

Meal	Food	Portion (g)	Energy content J	Energy content Cal
Breakfast	Sweet soup	250	840	200
	Cheese	30	290	70
	Meat	100	840	200
	Sausage	40	–	–
	or egg	one egg	420	100
	Honey or	20	250	60
	marmalade	30	–	–
	Butter	20	630	150
	Fruit	150	420	100
	Bread	100	1250	300
	Milk/yoghurt	250	630	150

Continued on next page

Competition phase

Before the start: some 2½ to 3 hours before the start the last meal should be taken. At the start the stomach should be neither empty nor full. For this reason the last pre-race meal should consist of foods that are easily digested and do not stay long in the stomach (see table on page 172). In general the following rules hold good for stomach emptying time:

☐ Small pieces of food do not stay in the stomach as long as large pieces of food, so every mouthful should be thoroughly chewed before swallowing.

☐ The greater the fat content of the food, the longer it stays in the stomach. For this reason lean foods are better, and fatty foods to be avoided.

☐ Animal foods generally stay longer in the stomach than vegetable foods. Therefore a decent steak stops you feeling hungry for a good while.

☐ Food which has a framework difficult for the stomach acids to break down stays longer in the stomach. Lentils, peas, beans and gherkins are examples of such foods.

Meal	Food	Portion (g)	Energy content J	Cal
Elevenses	Malt coffee	–	–	–
	or milk	250	630	150
	Bread, biscuits	50	630	150
	Fruit/muesli	150	630	150
	Marmalade or juice	30	290	70
Lunch	Soup	250	630	150
	Meat	150	1880	450
	Vegetables	200	630	150
	Potatoes	250	840	200
	Stewed fruit/dessert	200	840	200
	Fruit	100	210	50
	Juice	350	630	150
Tea	Tea with sugar	–	–	–
	Milk	one glass	420	100
	Cake	200	1460	350
	Stewed fruit/sweet	100	420	100
Dinner	Yoghurt/milk	250	840	200
	Meat	50	420	100
	Sausage	50	540	130
	Cottage or other cheese	100	420	100
	Egg or fish	50	460	110
	Vegetables	200	420	100
	Butter	30	920	220
	Bread	150	1460	350
	Stewed fruit/sweet	150	630	150
	Juice or milk	350	630	150

A time-honoured pre-race meal is a 200g lean steak, grilled or fried in the minimum amount of fat, served with bread, potatoes, rice or pasta. An old maxim was to take a gram of meat for every kilometre of the race distance. Some riders prefer about 150g of raw minced steak (tartare) and still others depend on muesli. A meal too rich in carbohydrates should be avoided, because it is not satisfying, and tends to have you feeling hungry again too quickly. Of course the topping-up of the glycogen stores should have been done in the pre-event phase and not just before the race. However, a carbo-hydrate-rich drink (about 150ml) a half-hour before the start is not a bad idea, although the energy contained (125–250 J, 30–60 Cal) is only quite low.

On principle you should never experiment with food on the day of a race, instead relying on feeding habits already tested in training. You have spent a long time preparing for the event, so don't put your victory chances in jeopardy by upsetting your diet.

☐ Concentrated sweet things (sugar, chocolate) and concentrated grape-sugar products delay the stomach emptying. The stomach empties at normal speed when sugar is only 5 to 6 per cent concentrated.

☐ Very cold and very hot drinks or food are emptied from the stomach more slowly than food at body heat.

☐ Stomach emptying is accelerated if during rest periods you lie on your right side.

Klaus-Peter Thaler at his
speciality: cyclo-cross.

Eating during a race

In road races of more than 80–100km, you must take food. In principle, however, the rider should have trained himself to complete a race with as little eating as possible. An optimal training of the fat metabolism processes during the training phase and the topping-up of the carbohydrate store during the pre-event phase should allow a long-term effort without much race eating, and you should begin feeding only after one or two hours. But in long road races eating is definitely necessary, to compensate for an energy consumption of more than 16,800 J (4000 Cal). The best method is to take a small amount of food every 30–45 minutes, but actual food needs will vary immensely according to the rider's training condition and his constitution. Some riders put this to good use, launching an attack when others are starting to take food.

Race food should not be too dry, so that it doesn't take much time to chew. Pure glucose isn't the best of race food, because it goes too quickly into the bloodstream and can trigger off a counter-effect of lowered blood sugar. It also increases thirst. The best things to take in your jersey pockets are carbohydrate-rich foods like bananas, slices of fruit, dried fruit, rice-cakes, custard tarts etc. In your feeding bottle you can have a drink based on oats or rice with added vitamins. Nowadays, however, there are drinks which are concentrates of carbohydrates and minerals, and these are important in hot weather, when the body's fluid and mineral balances have to be maintained. In track racing, where several events are ridden at intervals, it is best to take small helpings of easily-digested carbohydrate food during the time between events.

How long does food stay in the stomach?

Time in stomach	Food
1–2 hours	Water, coffee, tea, cocoa, broth, beer, soft-boiled egg, cooked rice, fresh-water fish.
2–3 hours	Boiled milk, coffee with cream, cocoa with milk, potatoes, mashed potato, tender vegetables, fruit, white bread, raw egg, hard-boiled eggs, scrambled eggs, omelettes, sea-fish, veal.
3–4 hours	Black bread, wholemeal bread, root vegetables, fried potato, kohlrabi, carrots, radishes, spinach, gherkins, apple, roast veal, beef steak (raw or cooked), ham, cooked tender chicken.
4–5 hours	Nuts, green cut beans, roast chicken and game, smoked meat, roast fillet of beef, salted herring.
6–7 hours	Streaky bacon, herring salad, mushrooms.
7–8 hours	Roast goose, tinned sardines.

Post-race phase

After a race, the preparation time for the next one begins immediately. In principle all the items used up during the race should be replenished as soon as possible. The regeneration process is thus accelerated, and the next training session can take place on the following day. Basically, don't drink much, even when you feel very thirsty, for once the stomach is filled with liquid there is no room for the carbohydrate-rich food which you should really be taking. Another thing is not to consume cold drinks after the race, because you are only inviting sore throats, stomach upsets and diarrhoea.

You should take your liquid in small amounts, and as near to body temperature as possible. The first meal should be taken 1½ or 2 hours after the race, perhaps a well-salted soup, a hot meat dish with carbohydrate-rich accompaniments and a dessert. Nutrition in the post-event phase is the transition into the training build-up phase.

Eating in stage races

There are special problems with stage-race feeding. Riders have only a few hours of regeneration between one finish and the next start. The lost energy must be replaced without delay. The luxury of long-term replacement is unthinkable in the circumstances. Stage riders use up some 21,000–25,000 J (5000–6000 Cal) daily, and need to replace some 5 to 8 litres of fluid, according to the temperature.

These quantities put great demands on the digestive system, which automatically limits the number of riders who are really cut out for stage racing. In some circumstances it is worthwhile increasing the fat intake, while decreasing the overall volume of nutrition. Concentrated foods have also proved their worth in stage races. Although in stage races the scientific rules of nourishment (high carbohydrate and protein intake, low fat intake) should be followed, in practice it is the rider's own hunger and thirst which regulate his food intake. So it is important to keep up the rider's appetite by offering a diet which is varied as well as nutritionally correct, and which takes into account his own tastes. There would be no point in giving someone a perfectly balanced and scientifically designed diet if they couldn't eat the food! Experienced athletes develop a natural instinct for selecting the right kind of foods.

Concentrated foods

Food concentrates contain more nutrients per unit volume than the naturally occurring food from which they are made. They are designed to complement, enrich and complete the normal basic diet, and to be easily consumed. With a daily demand of 21,000 J (5000 Cal) there can be problems satisfying it with normal foods; and special demands on stamina, strength and speed, as well as high sweat loss, can justify the application of concentrated foods. And sometimes there can be a loss of appetite during periods of intensive training, which gives an advantage to concentrates. However, these products should only be used to make your basic diet more complete.

You should never be diverted, after successful use of food concentrates, into using them instead of a normal healthy diet.

You should apply their use to the particular demand. For example, it is of little use to use a mineral supplement when you haven't had the sweat loss to justify it. It is also important to use them with an eye on the phasing of the diet.

We should essentially differentiate between concentrates which are predominantly carbohydrate, protein or minerals. Good concentrates also deliver vitamins in the right proportions. The ideal protein preparations offer the whole spectrum of vital amino acids. In cycle sport much successful use has been made of carbohydrate and mineral concentrates taken in the feeding bottle during long races. In addition, many riders have a spoonful or two of protein concentrate with their breakfast cereal. There are also special preparations for quicker recovery from intensive efforts. Concentrated foods have proved worthwhile in health pursuits, normal sports life and high-performance sport — if used sensibly.

Care of the body

The rider who through self-sacrifice, application and discipline has brought his body to a level of top performance, must naturally look after it. He should at least give his own body the kind of care he gives his racing machine. The better you look after your body, and the more correct a sporting life you lead, the more effective your training must be.

As I have already explained, a correct sporting lifestyle is a matter of enriching sleep, secure living conditions, a regular daily schedule, the right diet and the elimination of any factors which might diminish performance. In particular, it concentrates on regeneration, so that the next training session can take place as quickly as possible.

The morning should begin with **loosening-up exercises,** or **simple yoga and breathing exercises.** These promote suppleness, inner self-possession and concentration. With the help of breathing exercises stress situations can be mastered whenever they occur during the day, so that there is no undue loss of nervous energy.

The racing cyclist should take every opportunity to **harden** his body. It must be trained to withstand the weather: wind, cold and heat. He must be able to expose the skin of his body to any weather conditions, without illness as a result. Cold water applications, especially the morning cold shower, help in this respect — rub down with a rough towel. This kind of treatment toughens you against all kinds of infections.

For specific reasons, the racing cyclist is one of the cleanest of sportsmen. It is obvious that after his daily training run he bathes or showers. He should also lightly oil his skin (with baby oil or peanut oil, for instance). The crutch or **perineum area** should merit special attention because it must withstand all the friction of the saddle. After each race or training ride this part of the body should be scrupulously cleansed, and then lubricated with a camomile-glycerin lotion. If there are any signs of a blister, then the area should be treated with an antiseptic tincture such as Mercurochrome.

The chamois insert of the shorts

should be kept clean and soft. It can be treated with camomile-glycerin cream or with Cetavlon. If the chamois has become stiff or hard, it can be slightly dampened before applying the cream.

For hygienic reasons the racing cyclist **shaves his legs.** This is done with an electric razor. Shaven legs can be more easily massaged. For practical reasons, a disciplined rider will have a short haircut. If he sweats a lot, then the short haircut is simply more hygienic.

Part of body care is **regular bowel habits.** The body must rid itself of excess and unwanted materials this way. It is an important part of the sportsman's life style to leave plenty of time for the morning visit to the toilet. With good diet and regular training, riders are virtually never troubled by constipation.

If you have daily work commitments, then make sure to get up early enough to allow time for the morning exercises and body-care programme, for breakfast, and for the morning toilet visit.

Particularly important for recovery and for body-care generally are **massages.** Every rider should try to be massaged at least once a week. In fact, a rider can easily massage his own legs every day, using baby oil as a lubricant. Self-massage should be carried out before and after races, and a pre-race massage is especially important to loosen up the muscles. But be careful not to massage the legs with oil and embrocations which bring more blood to the skin surface, because this will be at the expense of the muscle blood supply, which is really essential.

In cold weather it should be enough to give the legs a thick coating of neutral oil, such as baby oil. In hot weather, you can use an oil containing peppermint or menthol, which has a cooling effect. If in the case of knee or back complaints you want a warming effect, then you can get special warming plasters from the chemist.

Finally, there is a form of **self-hypnosis,** which like yoga exercises helps to concentrate the mind on the body, making it more supple and following formulas to improve its performance. Once you have mastered the basics of this autogenous training, then you can go on to influence the effectiveness of training and eventually race results. Try repeating the following formulas:

- ☐ 'Today I will concentrate on training stamina (strength, speed, and so on)' — before every training session.

- ☐ 'I shall ride as elegantly as Didi Thurau' (or whoever you prefer) — before every technique session.

- ☐ 'I shall breathe more easily and in a more relaxed way' (in training or a race before a climb).

- ☐ 'I shall tackle this descent with full concentration and without nerves' (before a worrying descent).

- ☐ 'I shall go to the start relaxed and fully concentrated. That way I shall save energy and will be able to overcome my rivals' (to conquer pre-race nerves).

You can extend these formulas to cover every personal situation, and to bring out hitherto unexpected potential.

Preparation for competition

If you have had a systematic and appropriate training build-up, if you have followed the guidelines for a high-performance diet and for self-care, then you are ready for competition. The competition period is, just as the preparation period, divided into cycles: through build-up races you recognize your strengths and weaknesses, and improve your toughness. Then the training is structured to make good the identified weaknesses. In the third competition cycle you seek races with a higher degree of difficulty, until finally you are into the special preparation for the season's high point.

Road rider's preparation

The road rider should study the course profile and select the correct gear ratios. He should try to find out who his rivals will be, and to estimate their likely strength.
If possible, he should go over the circuit beforehand, preferably in a group of three to five, and at low speed. That is the best way to get to know the gradients, the state of the road, and any other peculiarities of the course. The rider should take all these facts into consideration when making his tactical plan, with the help of which he will be able to bring his skills and fitness to bear on the way the race develops. During the race he should be always placed so that he can cover the course with as little expenditure of energy as possible, yet can also keep a watchful eye on his opponents. He must have a clear idea of how he is going to tackle the tougher sections: climbs, descents, bends, rough surfaces. He must have worked out in his mind which breakaway attempts by which opponents he will want to share. He should also note the places where he himself might choose to make breakaway attempts, and whom he might like as breakaway companions. Taking into account the course, he can also work out his tactics for an eventual final sprint.
It is good to work out several different versions, just in case the race does not develop exactly as planned. It is obvious that before the race the rider should painstakingly check his machine and clothing, and make sure that he has everything else necessary with him — such as his crash-hat and his licence. That way he can go to the start with no undue anxiety.

Preparation for the trackman

The track rider must also prepare scientifically for his events, and they are usually less frequent than those of the roadman. He must concentrate on the opposition and work out a plan. Specially important for the track rider are nervous energy and concentration. The bike, the clothing, any other equipment, should all be ready. The track rider especially should find ways to heighten his concentration and ability to relax, such as yoga and autogenous training. The best preparation for racing is experience, and this can only be acquired through much competition. You must be self-critical of each performance, recognizing mistakes and weaknesses and setting out to eliminate them next time. Racing experience can never be replaced by theory.

Women in racing

Even in 1869 the first place-to-place races had women competitors astride machines weighing 50kg and having large iron-shod wheels. In the first international race from Paris to Rouen (123km) the then Miss America took 29th place.
This event took place on July 11, 1869, and in 1897 the first women's world championships took place in Belgium. In 1895 America's Annie Londonderry rode around the world, covering 28,000 miles in the process. From 1895 there were women's six-day races in England and the USA, although in fact they only raced for eight hours a day! Women's teams in mixed races often finished ahead of their male rivals.
In cycle sport it has already been shown that women are made for long and intensive endurance events. They have a lighter build and a thicker layer of subcutaneous fat than men. So it seems that anatomically they are predestined for endurance events. In running this has only been a recent discovery, for only

Beate Habetz, an expert on road and track.

in the last few years have women been allowed in marathon events. Women's racing in Britain had a good following even before it became internationally recognized. There had been official world championships in road racing, sprint and pursuit (3000m) since 1958. The first road championship was won by the Luxembourg rider Elsy Jacobs, who also set up the first women's world hour record with 41.347km. The most successful

woman rider until now has been the Belgian Yvonne Reynders, who was four times road champion and three time pursuit champion. Most successful track riders have been Russian.
In 1959 the first British medal at world level came from Beryl Burton, who took the track pursuit title at Rocourt, Belgium, the first of seven world titles she was to win on road and track. More recently, Bernadette Swinnerton took the road silver

medal in 1969 at Brno, and in 1975, Beryl's daughter Denise Burton took the pursuit bronze, coincidentally also at Rocourt. Most recent success has been the third-place medal of Mandy Jones, in 1980 at Sallanches, France.

Women can perform almost as well as men on a bike. They can do virtually every kind of cycle racing with some success. If they don't want top competition, then they can always go cycle touring. But in principle women are made for cycle sport. We shall see what improvements in performance the future brings, but in marathon and 100km running women have already shown just what their bodies are capable of.

Cycling veterans

In cycle racing veterans' events start at 35 or 40, when a man is still 'in his prime'. Anyone who wants to take out a veterans' licence can ride veterans' events. In recent years the number of racing veterans has greatly increased, and many veteran events get more entries than normal senior races.

Veterans train as hard as their juniors, and often harder. Veteran races are just as bitterly contested. Application to training is often greater, and there are several reasons for this. Most veterans raced some time ago; now they have had their families and the children are grown-up. They have made their careers. They recall their earlier racing years and now strive to reach those old performance levels. This is possible only with a relatively large amount of dedication to training. Most veterans manage to get in 50–100km each day, sometimes more. Veteran events are generally between 40 and 80km, which means one or two hours' racing. So correspondingly the race speed is quite high.

The average speed can be 40kph or more. Many veterans have years of experience behind them, and once they reach veteran age, are happy to 'ease off' into the veteran events. They find that the race speed is often higher at the start of veteran events than in normal senior races, and tactics and riding style are different too. Generally speaking the difference in ability of an amateur field is lower, so sprint finishes are more frequent, but not so dangerous because of the riders' wide experience. In fact, some amateur riders who have graduated to veteran class can get fed up with their style of riding and go back to senior events. But those who do settle down will often discover new enthusiasm for racing and in maintaining their physical condition. They tend to live a more regulated life, look for stability and have an eye on health. Without this form of self-discipline they have little chance of success in the veteran class.

Such is the proliferation of racing veterans that there are national competitions and championships for them, and even the 'World Cup' in Austria, which welcomes

A cycling veteran.

veterans from all over the world, separated into age groups from 30 to 80. It is an uplifting experience to see riders of 70 and 80 tackling the climbs — let us hope we are as fit when we're that old!

Cycle touring

If you look on cycling as part of a healthy life, rather than a competitive sport, then cycle touring is for you. Every national cycling federation has its touring department or section. Such tourists meet regularly and go on rides together, choosing pleasant roads and keeping the gears and speeds low. There is no suggestion of making big physical efforts. But there are organized touring rides, called Audax and Randonneur events, which are more sporting than leisure events. They are over predetermined courses on which an average speed of between 22 and 28kph must be maintained. There are usually check-points to make sure that riders cover the course, and group leaders who see that the speed is maintained. Usually at check-points there are refreshment facilities.

Apart from this mild form of competition, there is a charm in all cycle touring, the charm of companionship, of jointly improving health, of getting to know the countryside better than would be possible in a car, and making friends.

Cycle touring is the right start for all cyclists, and the Audax or Randonneur events can be an introduction to competition. Their low level of effort doesn't in fact separate them from races in the principles of training to be followed. Feeding should still be compact and effective, the way of life healthy, training regular. According to time available you can train for an hour two or three times a week. In this way you can stay really healthy and stave off the diseases of 'civilization' — blood pressure, circulation problems, heart disease, and metabolic problems such as diabetes and gout. Whoever rides a bike will probably stay healthy, or become healthy if he isn't already!

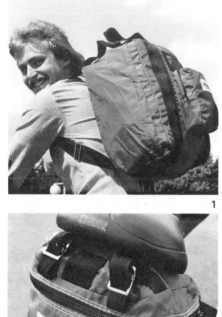

Luggage carrying on a bicycle.
1. Rucksack
2. Pannier bags
3. Saddlebag
4. Handlebar bag

1

2

3

4

Cycle touring, enjoyable in itself, is also an ideal introduction to the world of cycle sport.

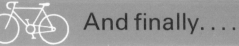

And finally....

Take a look around you. Anyone can try cycle sport, man or woman, young or old, all kinds of abilities or types of event. Anyone who regularly rides a bike has found a way to develop physically and mentally, to make more of themselves. For this reason the bicycle is an ideal sporting apparatus, for it gives its rider exercises which allow him to express himself and to improve himself. Whoever has enjoyed the ups and downs of a cycling career will never leave cycle sport and will always love it. He will always be reaching for his bike, to get back to Nature. He will be healthy, fit, and mentally fresh, no matter how old he is!